The Essential Guide to Selling Surplus Assets

New Solutions to a Universal Problem

Brin McCagg

TradeOut.com, Inc., Ardsley, New York

The Essential Guide to Selling Surplus Assets:
New Solutions to a Universal Problem

Executive Summary

Every company has surplus assets. It can be excess inventory, used plant equipment or unneeded office furniture – anything a company is not using in pursuit of its business. Surplus assets take up space and tie up capital, and they negatively impact your company's bottom line.

There are a range of traditional options available for disposing of surplus assets – resell them to another company or to a dealer, re-deploy them internally, barter them, donate them, etc. This Guide reviews the pros and cons of the various traditional options.

The Guide also reviews how the Internet is changing the way companies dispose of surplus. The driving force has been the evolution of Internet marketplaces, where thousands of businesses come together to transact business quickly and efficiently. Within these marketplaces, one method of sale that is being used with great success is the online auction. By tapping into the large pool of buyers at the marketplace, sellers can generate real competition and realize optimal market pricing on the items they sell.

TradeOut.com is the leading Internet marketplace for buyers and sellers of surplus assets. TradeOut.com enables companies to sell their surplus assets via an online auction or a fixed-price sale. The entire transaction gets completed online. The final section of the Guide details the benefits of selling surplus assets via an independent Internet marketplace such as TradeOut.com. These benefits include:

- True market pricing
- Fast transactions
- Control over the sale format
- Control over the terms of sale
- Precision targeting of buyers
- … and much more

The appendix of this Guide includes some valuable reference sections, including a directory of key trade and professional associations.

We hope that this Guide becomes a valuable and effective resource for the business community.

Table

Surplus marketplace

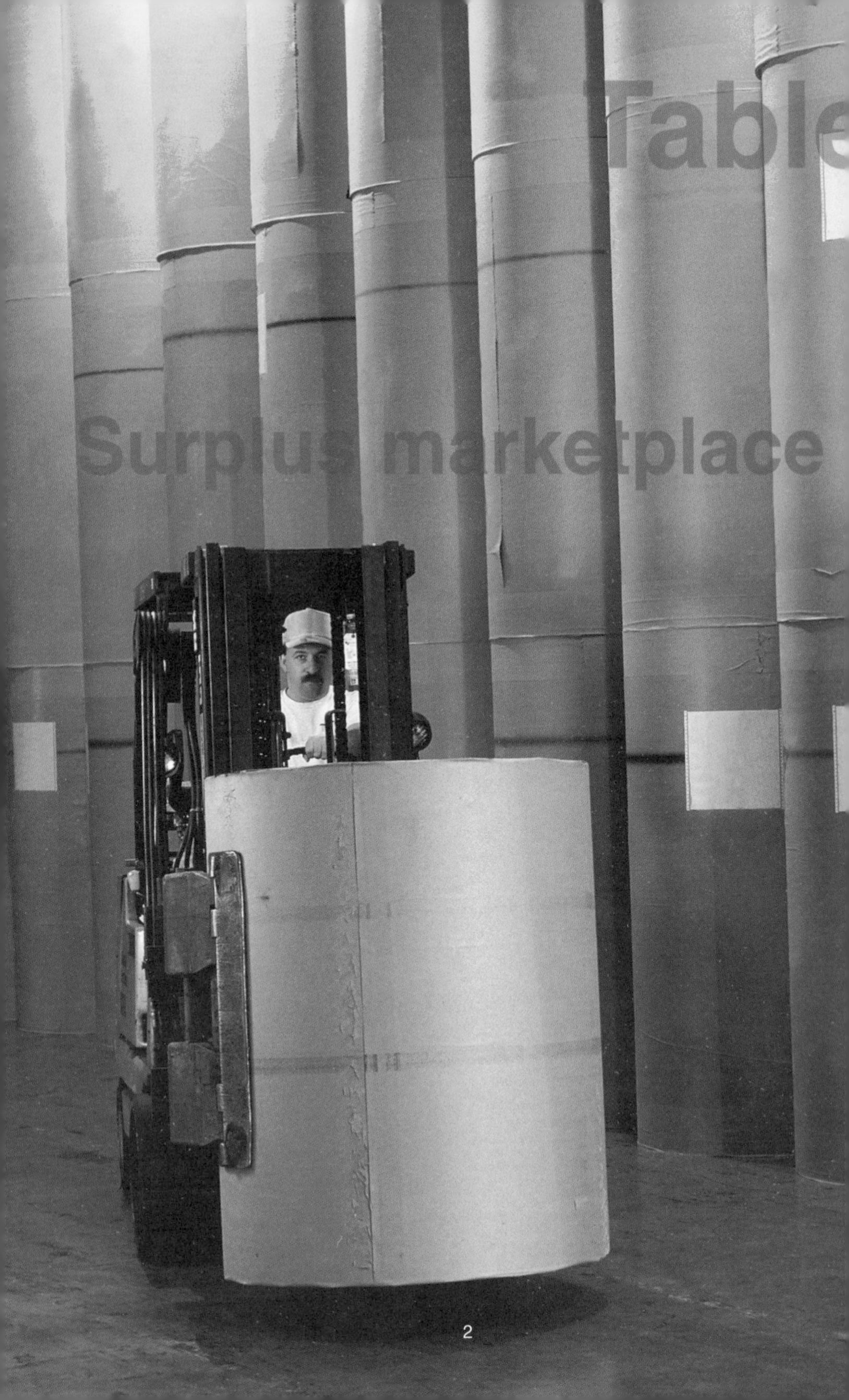

of Contents

Fast and efficient

duction

The Purpose of this Guide

Surplus. Every company – including yours – has plenty of it.

Surplus is anything in excess of what is required by your firm to conduct its primary business. Just take a look around your office, your plant floor or your warehouse, and you can't miss it. Obsolete office equipment. Idle factory machinery. Inventory overstocks. There is also surplus that you can't see, such as unused office space and excess factory capacity.

Although many companies don't pay much attention to surplus, there are very good reasons to be concerned about it. Surplus assets have a negative impact on your profits. They take up space and tie up capital. And managers use valuable time disposing of surplus.

The purpose of this Guide is to assist your company in effectively managing the disposal of surplus assets.

How this Guide was Created

TradeOut.com, an independent Internet marketplace where companies can buy and sell surplus assets, developed this Guide. The information contained in the Guide was derived from extensive research.

For primary research, TradeOut.com spoke at length with business professionals, across a wide range of industries, who are directly or indirectly involved in buying and selling surplus assets. This group includes CEOs, CFOs, manufacturing and supply chain executives, inventory managers, asset recovery managers, liquidators, equipment dealers, retailers, etc. The Guide incorporates many of their experiences and insights.

For secondary sources, TradeOut.com utilized studies by leading industry organizations, such as Forrester Research, the Institute for Management and Administration, the Center for Advanced Purchasing Studies, and the Investment Recovery Association. Key U.S. Government sources also were used.

This Guide reviews the various options available to you today for disposing of your company's surplus, including an extensive discussion of the TradeOut.com website. Every effort has been made to present the information in a fair and balanced manner. After you review the facts and examples contained in this Guide, we are confident you will conclude that TradeOut.com is one of your best options for disposing of surplus assets.

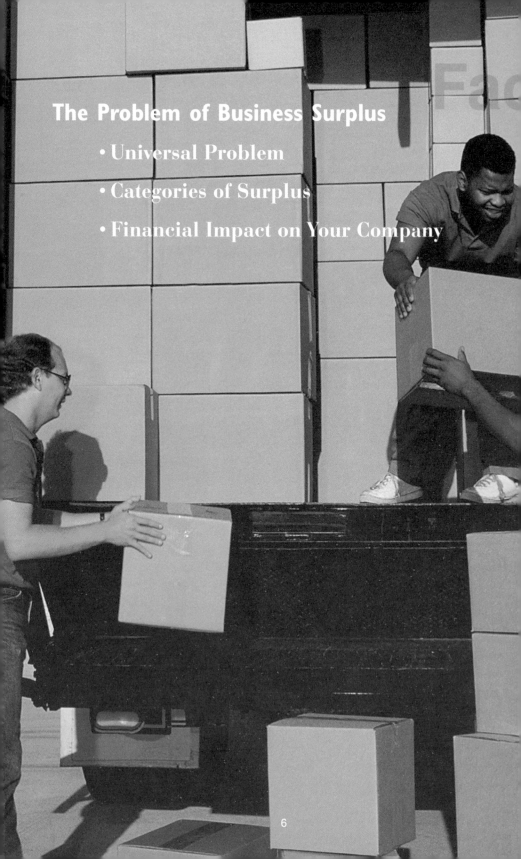

The Problem of Business Surplus

- Universal Problem
- Categories of Surplus
- Financial Impact on Your Company

The Problem of Business Surplus

A. Universal Problem

Whether you are the CEO, CFO or COO, or a Product Manager, Sales Manager or Plant Manager, you know about the problems created by surplus. Don't feel alone. It is estimated that the market for all business surplus is at least $350 billion annually.[1]

The problem is not going away. As the following table shows, despite concerted efforts by the business community to improve supply chain efficiency, inventory growth has actually outpaced sales growth.

INVENTORY AND SALES GROWTH TRENDS – U.S. COMPANIES[2]

MANUFACTURING SECTOR

	Year-Ending Inventory	Avg. Monthly Sales	Ratio
1990 ($ billions)	$399	$287	1.39
1996 ($ billions)	$438	$310	1.41
Change	+10%	+8%	+.02 pts.

RETAIL SECTOR

	Year-Ending Inventory	Avg. Monthly Sales	Ratio
1990 ($ billions)	$240	$184	1.30
1996 ($ billions)	$314	$203	1.55
Change	+31%	+10%	+.25 pts.

WHOLESALE SECTOR

	Year-Ending Inventory	Avg. Monthly Sales	Ratio
1990 ($ billions)	$196	$179	1.09
1996 ($ billions)	$256	$201	1.27
Change	+31%	+12%	+.18 pts.

It is reasonable to assume that a good chunk of that inventory consists of excess items. And managers seem to be feeling the pressure to get rid of it. A recent survey of inventory managers conducted by the Institute of Management and Administration (IOMA) found that "removing excess, obsolete or slow-moving inventory" has become their #1 most challenging task – by a 2:1 margin over the next most common response.[3]

[1] Statistical Abstract of the United States, 1998; World Bank.
[2] Statistical Abstract of the United States, 1998. Inventory figure is seasonally adjusted end-of-year data. Ratios are end-of-year seasonally adjusted inventories to seasonally adjusted sales.
[3] IOMA Inventory Reduction Report, June 1999 issue. The #2 problem was "improving lead times".

B. Categories of Surplus

Most business surplus falls into one of three main categories:
(1) finished goods inventory, (2) tangible operating assets, and
(3) capacity and space.

Finished goods inventory

Finished goods inventory consists of items
intended for resale by a manufacturer, distributor
or retailer. It can include consumer items, such as
electronics, gifts, toys, furniture, clothing,
housewares, health & beauty aids, food, hardware
and jewelry, or business items, such as
construction supplies and office equipment.

Examples of Finished Goods Inventory
• Manufacturer overruns
• Retail overstocks
• Discontinued and obsolete items
• Irregular and imperfect items
• Damaged goods
• Customer returns
• Label changes
• Promotional items

Some of the common factors contributing to inventory surplus are:

- forecasting inaccuracy
- new product introductions
- shifts in buyer preferences
- competitive activity
- cancelled orders

Operating assets

Operating assets are those items used by companies to manufacture goods, run their facilities or provide services.

Examples of Operating Assets
• Used factory machinery and parts
• Office furniture and equipment
• Material handling equipment
• Surplus manufacturing components
• Land and buildings
• Trucks and auto fleets
• Raw materials
• Store fixtures and equipment
• Supplies for MRO (maintenance, repair and operations)
• Shelving (display, stockroom, warehouse)
• Restaurant and food service equipment
• Salvage materials

There are a wide variety of reasons why some of these items become surplus:

- Corporate downsizing, leading to plant and office closures
- Relocation of facilities
- Upgrading and modernization of production facilities and offices
- Closure of retail facilities

Excess capacity and space

There is also a widely overlooked category of business surplus: excess capacity and space. It is not visible like other types of surplus, but it is no less important. Companies do not generate any return on their investment from the portion of the office, freight car or factory that is going unused. In these situations, firms have a tremendous opportunity to re-deploy this surplus capacity into revenue-generating activity.

Examples of Excess Capacity and Space
• Production capacity
• Shipping capacity
• Power transmission capacity
• Bandwidth capacity
• Excess office space
• Excess warehouse space

C. Financial Impact on Your Company

Business surplus is more than just an annoyance. Too much surplus creates a significant drag on your company's financial performance. It can reduce your earnings and eventually depress your company's stock price.

Here are some of the costs associated with surplus:

Sunk cost/opportunity cost. Surplus assets represent hard dollars that your company has invested. Too often a manager will dwell on the amount he or she has invested in an asset, and that becomes a barrier to selling it. However, in its surplus state, that asset has zero value to the company. Upon conversion of that asset to cash, the funds can be invested in a productive piece of equipment, used to pay down debt or put into the bank to generate interest.

Poor space utilization. Whether it is an old forklift sitting idle in the corner of a factory, or 500 discontinued computer monitors in a warehouse, surplus items take up space that could otherwise be used for productive, revenue-generating activity. Physical space costs money, and clogging it with unproductive assets does not help the productive part of your business.

Depreciation expense. Some assets can depreciate in value just sitting in a warehouse or storage yard. A 10-year-old bulldozer is worth more now than it will be in two years, even if it will not be used during that two-year period. In addition, the longer you hold onto surplus assets, the greater the risk that the assets will become obsolete due to technological changes, new products, etc. You can risk losing much of the value of your assets while you hold onto them.

Tracking expense. Companies use systems and people to keep track of surplus items. These activities add cost to a company's budget. The resources used for tracking surplus could be better deployed in more productive activities.

Maintenance costs. Some surplus equipment must be maintained while it sits idle to keep it in good operating condition.

Insurance costs. Surplus inventory and operating assets must be insured against damage or destruction.

Higher taxes. Surplus assets get counted as part of total assets, and in many jurisdictions they can increase a company's property tax base.

Here's an example of how those costs can mount up:

EXAMPLE: ABC Co. has 40,000 telephones, stacked on 200 pallets, sitting in its warehouse. It has been unable to sell them to any of its regular customers. ABC's cost to manufacture the telephones was $15/each, for a total sunk cost of $600,000. Assume that ABC could generate a 12% return on its money. Every month that ABC Co. holds onto the phones, it incurs the following costs:

Warehousing ($1/month per pallet)	$ 200
Inventory tracking (allocated monthly cost)	$ 500
Insurance ($.50/month per $1,000 of value)	$ 300
Financial opportunity cost ($600,000 x 12% return/12 months)	$ 6,000
Monthly cost	$ 7,000

Too much surplus also can adversely impact your company's Return on Assets (ROA). ROA is a key financial measure that is widely accepted in the business community as a measure of a company's performance. It is calculated as follows: ROA = Net Income ÷ Assets. The lower the amount of assets, the higher the ROA. The goal of most companies is to maximize net income while minimizing the level of assets.

Senior managers today are evaluated on ROA performance, and a large portion of their compensation can be tied to it. If that doesn't impact you directly, there's an excellent chance that it matters to your boss, or his or her boss. And that means he or she is likely to be very interested in what you are doing to improve ROA. In addition, if your company is publicly traded, you can bet that investors are monitoring your ROA closely. That means it can impact your stock price.

The following illustrates how eliminating surplus can improve ROA:

EXAMPLE: *Assume that DFX Inc. has revenues of $600 million, after-tax margins of 5%, inventory of $100 million and other assets of $50 million. Let's see what happens to ROA if DFX Inc. were to reduce its inventory levels by 5% and reduce its other assets by 1%.*

RETURN ON ASSETS

Current ROA	*($600 million x 5%) ÷ ($100 million + $50 million) = 20%*
Improved ROA *(5% reduction in inventory, 1% reduction in other assets)*	*($600 million x 5%) ÷ ($95 million + $49.5 million) = 21%*

As the example illustrates, even modest levels of asset reduction can increase ROA. In this instance, the +1 point gain in ROA reflects a +5% increase. If your company is looking to trim back its assets to improve ROA, then excess inventory and other surplus assets are the logical places to start.

To summarize, surplus assets have a significant negative impact on your company's financial performance. By implementing an aggressive program to dispose of surplus, you can improve your company's profits and other key financial indicators.

Disposing of Surplus

- Traditional Options
- Liquidation – The Most Common Optio

  1) Inefficient

  2) Slow and Time-Consuming

  3) Channel Conflict

14

Disposing of Surplus

A. Traditional Options

Once you've decided that you should get rid of surplus assets, you have many choices. You can:

- resell directly to other companies
- re-deploy assets to other locations within your company
- return the assets to the vendor
- trade-in the assets to a dealer
- arrange a barter deal
- donate the items for a tax deduction
- reclaim the parts for use in other equipment
- demolish or scrap the items
- turn the goods over to an auction house
- sell the goods to a liquidator or dealer

The final option, sale to a liquidator or dealer, is the solution used most often. We'll explore the liquidation market in depth in the next section.

Let's first review the other options:

Resell directly to other companies:

If you want to undertake a direct sale to another company, you have many choices. If you are disposing of operating assets, such as processing equipment, you might be able to sell to another manufacturer. For excess inventory, you may find wholesale distributors or discount retailers who are interested in your products.

But how do you find these companies? For most surplus assets, there might be hundreds of companies potentially interested in buying them from you at a fair price. However, finding the right ones, at the right time, is akin to finding a needle in a haystack. Locating them will require a serious allocation of time and manpower. And once that is accomplished, you still have to go through the negotiation process.

Therefore, while a direct sale might generate more revenue than some of the other disposal options, it also will require the greatest use of your internal resources.

Re-deploy the assets

Large companies with multiple locations often re-deploy assets from one location to another. The bigger your company, the more likely it is you can find someone within your firm who is interested in taking your surplus.

However, internal communications are not always perfect. Many large companies still use old-fashioned methods – like fax and hard copy listings – to communicate with facilities around the world. Without a well-developed Intranet, you may not be able to communicate the relevant information to your internal buyers in a timely fashion.

And even if communications are not a problem, you are still restricting your pool of buyers by not tapping into the open market. There could be very strong demand for your surplus among outside companies, and you won't know about it if you consider only the internal transfer option.

Despite these limitations, many managers still feel that "keeping things in the family" is the best option for their companies. In some instances, it is. But as the example below illustrates, that doesn't always hold true:

EXAMPLE: Global Corp. operates chemical processing plants in 23 countries. Its Canadian division is closing down a plant in Toronto and selling off all of the equipment. Jeff, the chief plant engineer, compiles a list of equipment that is available and sends the list via email to plant managers at Global's other manufacturing locations.

Carlos, who runs the Mexico City plant, notices that Jeff is selling a filtration system. The intra-company transfer price has been set at $300,000, based on the system's current book value. Carlos already has budgeted $750,000 to purchase a similar used system on the open market. If he buys this one from the Canadian division, Carlos' division will be able to use the difference on other capital projects. So Carlos contacts Jeff and tells him that he wants it.

This transaction seems to be a "no-brainer" for Global Corp., right?
Let's take a closer look.

It will cost $40,000 to ship the system from Canada to Mexico on three
flatbed trucks. Jeff and Carlos agree to split the cost – but no matter
which one of them pays for it, it will cost Global Corp. $40,000.

Also, there were some third parties, closer to their respective plants, with
which Jeff and Carlos could have done business if they had chosen to
explore other options. ABC Manufacturing Co., based in Buffalo, had been
searching for a used filtration system. ABC would have been willing to pay
Jeff $775,000 for the equipment, and also absorb the shipping costs.

Carlos also had other options. XYZ Systems, a used equipment dealer in
San Antonio, was selling a similar system for $725,000. Carlos' budget of
$750,000 would have covered the purchase price and the $15,000
shipping cost.

Let's compare the financial outcome for Global in both scenarios:

CANADIAN DIVISION

	Internal Transfer	External Transaction
Revenue from Sale	$300,000	$775,000
Shipping Cost	($20,000)	-------
Net Revenue	$280,000	$775,000

LATIN AMERICAN DIVISION

	Internal Transfer	External Transaction
Purchase Price	($300,000)	($725,000)
Shipping Cost	($20,000)	($15,000)
Total Cost	($320,000)	($740,000)

Net Financial Impact for Global	($40,000)	$35,000

As you can see, an intra-company transfer is not always the best
solution. Beware of the often-overlooked costs associated with an
internal transfer. Shipping equipment great distances is expensive.
And selling the assets outside of the firm can often yield higher net
revenue than an internal transfer.

Return the asset to the vendor

Vendors accept returns in some situations. For example, if you are a retailer or a wholesale distributor, you may be able to return new, unsold merchandise to the manufacturer. But what will you get for it?

Unless you are a huge customer, with tremendous clout, it is very unlikely that the vendor will give you a complete (dollar for dollar) refund. Instead, if you get a refund at all, you are likely to receive only a small portion of the purchase price. In many instances, you may be better off reselling the assets yourself.

Trade-In

Remember the last time you bought a new car and traded in your old car at the same time. You probably were shocked at how little the dealer offered you. Your old car was still in great condition, and you thought it was worth more.

That is exactly what you will encounter when you try to sell your old equipment to a new equipment dealer. What you need to remember is that used equipment is not the dealer's primary business, so the dealer may not have a quick means of turning around and reselling your equipment. Because your equipment will not have high liquidity in his hands, he can not afford to pay you very much on a trade-in.

Barter

Barter is the oldest form of business-to-business transaction, and it is still practiced widely. In traditional barter, a company trades assets for other assets. If you can barter your surplus for something you really need, and you are confident that what you will get in return has a higher value than what you could get from selling your surplus for cash, this is a very attractive  proposition. Needless to say, these opportunities are hard to find.

A different type of barter that emerged in the 1990's involves the trading of assets for trade credits, which can then be used to purchase things like air travel or advertising media. This type of barter is quite appealing in concept, and some companies have taken advantage of it.

However, bartering for credits has never really lived up to the hype. Many companies have been left holding credits they can't use. We spoke with one large company that traded excess inventory for credits that could be used to buy advertising time on daytime television. Unfortunately, most of the firm's products are targeted to men, who tend to watch very little TV during that time period. Accordingly, those credits have little utility to the company.

In addition, the value of the credits provided in return for the assets is often grossly overstated because they are usually bartered at full cost. As a result, media credits supposedly valued at $200,000 may be worth only $20,000 in the current market. Therefore, bartering for credits can be a risky financial transaction and has fallen out of favor with a majority of firms.

Donation for a tax deduction

Charitable contributions can be a viable solution in some situations. U.S. Internal Revenue Code Section 170 provides a tax deduction for certain qualifying donations of assets.

Internal Revenue Code Section 170(e)(3) details specific provisions governing contributions of inventory. As a general rule, you can claim as a charitable contribution the fair market value of the property, reduced by one-half of the amount of gain if the property had been sold at fair market value. This provision applies only to certain types of property and requires that the donated property be used to care for the ill, the needy or children.[4]

---

[4]26 USC Sec. 170(e)(3). Please consult your tax advisor before proceeding with any such transaction. TradeOut.com makes no representation and assumes no liability for the accuracy of the information or examples contained herein.

EXAMPLE: Maxwell Industries has two truckloads of surplus paper plates and cups. The items cost $10,000 to produce. The current fair market value of the goods is $13,000. The company doesn't want to go through the effort to sell the surplus, so it decides to donate the goods to some local churches for use in soup kitchens.

Maxwell could claim a charitable contribution as follows:

$13,000   *fair market value*
- $ 1,500   *1/2 of the $3,000 gain if Maxwell had sold the goods*
$11,500

Assuming that Maxwell can deduct the full amount of the contribution, and assuming a 40% federal corporate tax rate, the deduction is worth $4,600 to Maxwell. Accordingly, Maxwell will incur a loss of $5,400 on the transaction ($10,000 cost of goods less $4,600). And that doesn't even take into consideration the $3,000 lost profit opportunity.

(Note: This example is provided for illustrative purposes only. Please consult your tax advisor before proceeding with any such transaction.)

Donations can be a worthwhile option. You can do some good for others and get rid of that nagging surplus of yours at the same time. But bear in mind that you will not recoup most of the value of your assets. From a purely financial perspective, a charitable donation may not be the answer.

Reclamation

If your surplus equipment is similar to other equipment still in use by your company, a good option may be to dismantle the surplus equipment and use the parts for ongoing maintenance of the working equipment. That route can sometimes be more cost effective than purchasing replacement parts on the open market.

Scrap/Demolition

You can sell your surplus assets for scrap. It may be the quickest solution – but also the least profitable. You will get virtually nothing in return for your assets. And in some cases, when your assets have little or no scrap value, it actually will cost you money out-of-pocket to have another company come and take them away.

Auction

Auctions are a great way to dispose of your business surplus. Because auctions create open competition for goods, the auction format will generate higher selling prices than fixed-price sales.

You can hold your own live auction, but that is no small undertaking. Unless you really know what you are doing, you will be better off using an established auction house to run the auction, either on your premises or at their location.

However, there are some limitations of traditional, live auctions that you should bear in mind:

- An auction will generate better selling prices for you only if it attracts an adequate number of qualified and interested buyers. The auction house must market the auction properly to ensure that enough of the right people attend and participate.

- As a seller you will pay auctioneers a hefty commission, usually 10-20% of the selling price. You also could incur other big costs. If you are not conducting the auction on your own premises, you will bear the expense of shipping the goods to the auction site. If the goods don't sell, you also will have to pay to ship them back to your facility, and your goods could be damaged during transport. Also, it takes significant management time to supervise this process.

B. Liquidation – The Most Common Option

You probably use a variety of methods for disposing of surplus assets – perhaps some that we just reviewed. But if your company is like most, you most frequently sell your surplus to liquidators and dealers.

Liquidation firms tend to deal either in excess finished goods inventories or in surplus operating assets. Those that deal in finished goods inventories are also known as jobbers or closeout dealers. They purchase large quantities of goods (i.e. pallets, truckloads) from manufacturers and distributors, and then resell them in smaller lots to wholesalers or discount retail stores.

The firms that buy surplus operating assets, such as plant machinery or office equipment, are known as equipment dealers. They resell the assets to manufacturers and other end users.

Liquidators and dealers play a valuable intermediary role. Many of them specialize in particular industries (e.g., grocery products, office furniture, mining equipment), and they can have vast knowledge of those industries and the key players in the business. That enables them to act as a conduit between companies looking to sell surplus and companies looking to buy that same type of surplus. Because liquidators generally take ownership and possession of the assets, and bear the associated risks and costs, they charge a premium to sellers – in the form of lower purchase prices.

Selling your surplus to liquidators seems fairly simple on the surface. You just look in a directory, find five or six liquidators, call them and then take the best offer. You get a fair price, the liquidator takes the goods off of your hands and everyone is happy. Right?

As many of you already know, it is not quite that simple – as we will see below.

1) Inefficient

In an efficient market, information is plentiful and flows freely. Sellers can easily find buyers who want their products, and buyers can easily find sellers who are selling the types of products they want.

Efficient markets also stimulate competition. When there are numerous buyers with genuine interest in an item, competition will help establish the market value for the goods. The more interested buyers you have, the more likely it is that the optimal market price will be realized.

Judging by those criteria, the liquidation market is far from efficient. In the current market (1) the liquidators are highly fragmented, (2) relevant information is not easily accessible, and (3) there is insufficient competition for surplus items among liquidators.

TradeOut.com estimates that there are well over 10,000 liquidation firms and surplus dealers in the United States, covering the gamut of industries from aerospace to zippers. But if your company is like most, you probably do business with just a few liquidators and dealers on a regular basis. What might surprise you is that if you wanted to find additional liquidation firms to buy your surplus, you could have a tough time finding them.

There are no directories that provide comprehensive, meaningful information on liquidation firms. New referrals tend to come slowly. And your current liquidators are unlikely to share information about their sources with other liquidation firms, so new liquidation firms can't easily get in touch with you. So you end up selling to the same liquidators, again and again. What happens in that situation? Your regular liquidators realize that they have little competition for your items. As a result, they have no reason to pay you a fair price for your surplus.

Now, let's assume you decide to do the legwork to find some additional liquidators who might want your surplus. When you find them, there's a good chance they won't be the right kind of liquidators – they don't specialize in the type of surplus you have, but they want to buy it anyway. What happens in that scenario? Because these liquidators do not have well-developed channels and connections for reselling the items, they are unable to offer you a fair market price for the items.

In both situations, you are likely to sell your surplus for less than it is worth. The inefficiency of the market prevents you from easily linking up with the right kinds of buyers.

Let's take a look at some examples of this inefficiency in action:

EXAMPLE: Dealing with Too Few Liquidators

Sigma Corp. manufactures athletic shoes for discount stores. Last month, Sigma received a large order from a major customer, Big C, for 15,000 pairs of kids athletic shoes. Sigma produced them at a cost of $120,000 ($8/pair), and was planning to sell them to Big C for $225,000 ($15/pair).

Shortly before the shoes were shipped, Big C filed for bankruptcy. Sigma stopped shipment, and now it has 15,000 pairs of blue and red sneakers sitting in three trailers behind its distribution center.

Joe, the controller at Sigma, wants to sell them quickly and recoup as much as possible. He picks up the phone and calls VF Sneaker Liquidators – a firm to which Sigma often has sold surplus inventory in the past.

VF buys and sells only surplus athletic shoes, and has great expertise in the athletic shoe industry. In fact, the principals at VF already have tentative deals with several small discount retailers to resell

Sigma's shoes for a total of $150,000 ($10/pair). Yet VF offers Joe only $50,000 ($3.33/pair) for the shoes. That figure represents 22% of Sigma's normal wholesale selling price and only 42% of Sigma's $120,000 manufacturing cost. Joe doesn't have any other immediate options, and he reluctantly accepts the $50,000 offer.

How can VF offer Sigma such a low price? And why would Sigma accept that offer? VF knows the industry very well, and it is confident that Sigma doesn't sell its surplus to other athletic shoe liquidators. VF also keeps its merchandise sources to itself, so its competition is not aware that Sigma has goods to sell. Finally, VF believes that Sigma can't find other athletic shoe liquidators quickly and easily.

So even though VF can afford to pay Sigma a much higher price, it offers only $50,000. It doesn't **have to** pay any more due to the lack of competition – which has been caused by inadequate information.

How did Sigma Corp. make out in this transaction?

	Planned Sale to Big C	Sale to VF Liquidators
Sigma's Production Cost	($120,000)	($120,000)
Selling Price	$225,000	$50,000
Profit/(Loss) on Transaction	$105,000	($70,000)

Sigma Corp. was expecting to make a profit of $105,000 on the original transaction, and instead ended up losing $70,000 – a negative swing of $175,000.

EXAMPLE: Dealing with the Wrong Liquidators

Forge Co. produces faucets for residential use. Due to a recent slowdown in new home construction, the demand for faucets has flattened out, leaving Forge with excess warehouse inventory on 10 of its SKUs. Altogether, Forge is sitting on 20,000 pieces, at a cost of $200,000 ($10/each), and a wholesale price of $400,000 ($20/each).

A number of liquidation firms around the country specialize in bathroom and plumbing fixtures, but Alison, Forge's inventory manager, doesn't know any of them because Forge has not needed to liquidate any inventory previously. Alison thumbs through some local business journals and finds three liquidators – firms A, B and C. These firms buy and sell all types of general merchandise.

Because there are three firms involved, Alison expects the competition to generate a fair price. However, none of these liquidators knows the surplus fixture market very well. They are general merchandise closeout firms and they don't have regular customers to whom they can easily resell the faucets. For these three firms, there is some risk in buying the faucets. They are taking on Alison's problem, and it could ultimately turn into their own problem. That limits the price they are willing to offer. So, despite the apparent competitive situation, the best offer that Alison receives for the lot is $120,000, 30% of the wholesale price, from Liquidator C.

The real problem is that none of these firms is the "right" buyer. The "right" buyer in this case would be a firm that specializes in fixtures, or one that knows of excellent resale opportunities before making the purchase. Such firms can offer a higher price because they have lower risk. But because of the fragmentation of the surplus market and the inadequate flow of information, Forge Co. can't easily find these "right" buyers. And, conversely, these "right" buyers are not aware that Forge Co. has faucets to sell.

If Alison proceeds with the sale to Liquidator C, Forge will lose $80,000.

EXAMPLE: Dealing With the "Right" Liquidators

Now, let's change that scenario slightly. Assume that Alison is able to locate and contact two firms that specialize in buying surplus fixtures, (D and E), plus a bathroom fixture buyer for a major home improvement retailer (F). The faucets are more valuable to these new buyers because they don't carry as much risk. These new buyers are the "right" buyers that we discussed above. They are in a better position to offer Alison a fair price.

In this new scenario, Forge Co. benefits from some real competition. The high offer comes from Firm E, which knows of a buyer outside of the country to whom it can resell the faucets right away, for $15/each. So Firm E offers Alison $240,000 ($12/each) – a fair price – and E makes a quick $60,000 profit on the resale.

Let's compare the two scenarios we just discussed:

	Proposed Sale to Liquidator C	Sale to Firm E
Forge Co.'s Cost of Goods	($200,000)	($200,000)
Selling Price	$120,000	$240,000
Forge Co.'s Profit/(Loss)	($80,000)	$40,000

In the second scenario, Forge was able to connect with the right kind of closeout firm and realize a $40,000 gain, a swing of +$120,000 vs. the previous scenario.

Finding the "right" buyers is not easy, but it can be worth your effort to track them down in some cases. However, if you do find them, you still have to contend with a very outdated selling process in today's liquidation market.

2) Slow and Time-Consuming

Liquidating surplus is no easy task. Be patient and be prepared to devote considerable time to it. You will have to manage the back-and-forth communications and the negotiation process, and expend great effort doing so.

EXAMPLE: Mason Corp. is a soft drink bottler. Bill, plant manager at Mason's Cleveland facility, has recently installed a new high-speed filling line. The previous line was slower, but it still functions well and it has been crated and moved to a corner of the warehouse while Bill tries to sell it. Bill estimates that it should fetch $500,000 in the secondary market.

Using some legwork, Bill has compiled a list of six used equipment dealers that specialize in beverage equipment. He sends each of them a fax with a description of the old filling line. Here's what happens over the next few days. [See if any of this sounds familiar to you.]

Firm A calls Bill and leaves a voicemail message requesting more information. Bill puts together a package and sends it out. Firm B sends Bill a "low-ball" offer via fax. Bill writes back a quick note saying that the offer is too low. Firm B sends Bill another offer – still too low.

Firm C doesn't respond at all, so Bill re-sends the original fax. The owner of Firm D contacts Bill via telephone. He appears interested, and after a twenty-minute conversation, he says he'll get back to Bill – but he doesn't. The people at Firm E also seem interested, and they request some additional specs via fax.

Firm F is located in Tampa. The principals are interested and would like to inspect the equipment in Bill's warehouse. They try to get Bill to agree to pay for their travel costs, which Bill declines to do. Bill makes arrangements to have the equipment uncrated for inspection, and clears his calendar so that he can meet with representatives from Firm F when they visit the following week.

Seems like a lot of effort to sell a piece of equipment. Just think how Bill feels. And that was just the first week! During the next two weeks, Bill will have follow-up communications with several of the firms, some in person, some via phone, some via fax, and some via email. And Bill will negotiate with several of them over price, payment terms and shipping terms – until he gets an acceptable offer. In all, Bill will conduct six separate, bilateral negotiations.

And, in case you forgot, Bill still has a plant to run.

3) Channel Conflict

At times it seems that you are gambling when you sell your surplus inventory into the liquidation market. It's a bit like roulette. Round and round it goes, where it ends up nobody knows. Once you sell it to a liquidator it is out of your control – and you hope that it doesn't end up in the wrong place:

> *Your company produces premium cologne that retails for $30 a bottle in department stores. You have a bit of an overstock after Christmas and you decide to sell off some of your surplus to an export liquidator for $10 a bottle, which covers your cost. The liquidator promises that the cologne will be exported to Latin America. Congratulations! You just solved your surplus problem. But then you learn that your buyer didn't export the goods after all. He resold them to a big discount warehouse in the Northeast – which is now selling your cologne, to your consumers, for $13 a bottle.*

This is called diversion. Goods intended for retail sale in a particular location end up being diverted to an entirely different – and often inappropriate – location. If that happens too often, it will anger your current distributors and retail customers, and it can erode the value of your brand.

> *Your firm sells hammers to your biggest customer, Home Haven, for a wholesale price of $8 each. Home Haven retails the hammers for $12 each. You are about to introduce a new model and you want to clear out the inventory of the old ones. Of course, you first offer the closeout stock to Home Haven, but it declines.*
>
> *You have no takers for the hammers among your regular customers, so you sell them to a jobber for $4 each. The jobber quickly resells them to Closeout World – which has several locations right next door to Home Haven. Closeout World is now selling them for $7 each – $1 less than Home Haven's wholesale cost. Home Haven is not happy.*

These are just a couple of examples of what is broadly referred to as "channel conflict". If you are going to do business in the traditional liquidation market, it is bound to happen from time to time. However, there are certain things you can do to minimize channel conflict:

- Make sure you are dealing with reputable buyers. Check their D&B rating to see if they are legitimate. Also, try to obtain references from other firms with which they have transacted business.

- Be very clear, right upfront, about any resale restrictions. Incorporate the restrictions explicitly into your terms of sale.

- Don't "dump" your goods. If you sell your surplus goods too cheaply just to unload them, you create a lot of room for the goods to be resold over and over again before they get to a retail location. When that happens, they invariably end up in the wrong places.

Business

E-Commerce Brings Big Changes in Business-to-Business Markets

- Growth of E-Commerce – and What it Means for Your Busine
- Evolution of Intermediaries
- Internet Marketplaces
- Online Auctions

E-Commerce Brings Big Changes in Business-to-Business Markets

A. Growth of E-Commerce –
and What it Means for Your Business

The growth of business-to-business transactions has been explosive, and is projected to accelerate in the next few years:

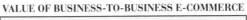

VALUE OF BUSINESS-TO-BUSINESS E-COMMERCE

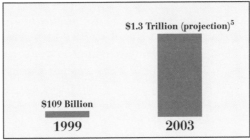

$1.3 Trillion (projection)[5]

$109 Billion

1999   2003

You can not pick up a newspaper or business journal without reading a headline about how e-commerce will change the face of business. Many well-respected business experts have likened the advent of e-commerce to a second industrial revolution.

That is a pretty bold comparison, but it is probably accurate. The Internet <u>will</u> fundamentally alter the way your company does business in the future – if it hasn't done so already. Every aspect of your firm's operations, from purchasing to order fulfillment, from advertising to customer service, will be impacted – for the better – by the Internet.

The reasons are obvious. The Internet can be used to transmit meaningful, real-time information to thousands of people simultaneously. Business transactions can occur with greater speed and lower manpower costs. All of these factors create tremendous efficiency.

E-Commerce

[5]Forrester Research

B. Evolution of Intermediaries

Prior to the emergence of the Internet, a wide range of intermediaries played a key role in our economy. These intermediaries included travel agents, stockbrokers and even retail stores. These firms provided an important linkage between large groups of buyers and sellers, because there were no alternate means for buyers and sellers to transact business. However, many of these intermediaries have found that the efficiency of the Internet has made their roles less important today – even obsolete in some cases.

Does that mean that the Internet eliminates the need for all business intermediaries? Not at all. Actually, there is a tremendous need for the right kind of intermediaries. For e-commerce to thrive, it is not as simple as giving everyone Internet access and just setting them loose. How will buyers and sellers find each other? What is needed are central hubs where many buyers and sellers can come together and transact business quickly and efficiently. A new breed of Internet marketplaces will replace the intermediaries of the past.

C. Internet Marketplaces

Online marketplaces foster market efficiency within a particular industry or market. What they share in common is the following:

- Bring together thousands of widely dispersed buyers and sellers, providing truly global reach.

- Act as 'infomediaries' by facilitating the distribution and flow of information in the form of data, text, photographs, video and sound.

- Provide an environment for establishing optimal market pricing.

- Streamline buying and selling, which accelerates transactions and reduces transaction costs.

We already have seen online marketplaces establish themselves in some consumer markets. Stock trading is one example. In the past, investors had no choice but to trade securities through full-service brokers. Now, investors have other options, including Internet brokers, for executing trades. These Internet brokers link millions of investors to the securities market quickly and cost effectively. And because of their low overhead, they can charge as low as $7 per trade, compared to $100 or more for a traditional firm. For investors who don't require the added services of a full-service broker, this is an easy decision.

The travel industry provides another example of how traditional intermediaries are being replaced by online marketplaces. Only a few years ago, travelers either had to purchase airline tickets through a travel agent, or else deal with each airline individually – a very time-consuming process. Now, a number of websites have assumed the intermediary role. An individual can use these sites to obtain information on fares and availability from all major airlines simultaneously, and then purchase the tickets online. These sites bring buyers and sellers together to exchange information and transact business quickly and efficiently.

Online business-to-business marketplaces have emerged only recently, but they are quickly becoming the preferred transactional venue for many companies. Some business-to-business marketplaces focus on goods within a single industry, such as steel or chemicals. These are referred to as "vertical" marketplaces. On the other side of the spectrum are "horizontal" marketplaces. They serve companies across multiple industries, and often focus on an area that is common to all of those industries – such as surplus assets. Like consumer marketplaces, business-to-business marketplaces serve an intermediary role that is essential for truly efficient e-commerce.

D. Online Auctions

Within Internet marketplaces, companies buy and sell products and services in a variety of ways. The most common method is the straight fixed-price sale. Sellers list their goods at a given price, and buyers make the purchase through the website.

However, the sale format that has really caught the attention of the business community is the online auction. This follows on the heels of the tremendous

growth of online auctions via consumer marketplaces. Only a few short years ago, online auctions did not even exist. Yet it is now estimated that by 2002, goods and services valued at $52.6 billion will sold via online business-to-business auctions.[6]

What explains the phenomenal growth of online auctions? The answer is simple. Sellers love auctions because buyers bid against each other simultaneously, and that creates competition. Buyers love auctions because it gives them access to many of the things they are looking for in a single, convenient location.

And when enough of the right buyers participate in an auction, it creates a truly competitive environment. Sellers are more likely to realize a fair market price from the sale. Therefore, under the right conditions, auctions can harness the power of competition to establish optimal market pricing. Accordingly, **an online auction can be an ideal avenue for selling your surplus assets.**

If you want to auction your surplus assets online, there are three types of websites for you to consider: (1) your own company-operated auction site; (2) vertical marketplaces; and (3) horizontal (multi-industry) marketplaces.

Auctions at company-operated sites:

There are a number of auction sites that are operated by manufacturers or distributors trying to auction their own surplus (e.g., Lucent, Ingram Micro). These sites are not true marketplaces, however, because they only include a single seller and don't provide buyers with access to a wide range of items and services.[7]

---

[6] Forrester Research

[7] There are also a number of sites operated by online liquidation firms (e.g., uBid.com, Onsale.com). These firms auction off surplus items to consumers that they have purchased from manufacturers and distributors. If you are considering selling your surplus to one of these online liquidation firms, bear in mind that some of these firms "cherry pick" only the best of your surplus assets, and they often retain the right to return what they don't sell. In addition, they may not pay you any more for your assets than you would realize by selling to a traditional liquidator. As a result, the online liquidation firm - not your company - will reap all of the aforementioned benefits of an online auction.

Also, beware of some dealer-operated sites that purport to conduct online auctions, when in reality they are not running auctions at all. These sites solicit and accept "bids" online, but the bid is really nothing more than an email communication of an offer from a buyer to the dealer. These sites also accept offers via phone and fax, and, in the end, the deals still get done via traditional back-and-forth negotiation. Also, potential buyers are not given information as to what other buyers already have offered, which eliminates the key competitive element that characterizes a true, online auction.

As a seller, operating your own site does have some advantages. You maintain complete control over the site, and you avoid paying commissions on what you sell. But before you take the plunge and set up your own auction site, there are few things you should think about:

- You will need auction software. Expect to pay at least $100,000 for a good off-the-shelf program, and several times that for installation and maintenance. Remember also that you will need to buy new versions of the software if you want the latest functionality. And because you won't have access to the source code, you will have to rely entirely on the software provider to fix any bugs. You lose control over how quickly bugs get fixed.

  If you choose instead to develop your own proprietary software, you will need to hire a world class software development team. Auction software is extremely complex. If you outsource the project, be prepared to pay anywhere from $500,000 to $5,000,000, depending upon what features and functionality you desire.

  In either case, your company will need to invest in expensive servers and database software. In addition, you'll need a full time technical staff to operate and troubleshoot the system. Don't be seduced by the allure of running your own auction site. It is no small undertaking.

- "If you build it, they will come." It's a great old saying. But it is only true in the movies. Getting the site built and running is only the first step. You will need to invest large sums behind comprehensive and sustained marketing efforts to drive buyers to the site.

- No matter how hard your company works to bring buyers to its site, a single company site will never attract as many buyers as a strong vertical or horizontal marketplace. You won't be able to realize the economies of scale enjoyed by larger, independent community sites. As a result, it is unlikely that you'll be able to make the necessary investment to develop and maintain first-rate functionality and scalability for your site.

E-Commerce

35

The following summarizes the pros and cons of operating your own auction site:

	PROS	CONS
Software Purchase	Moderate Expense ($100,000)	No access to source code
Software Development	Control source code	$500M to $5MM cost
Site Maintenance		$1MM ongoing cost
Sales Commissions	No commissions	
Marketing		Heavy investment needed to attract buyers
Buyers		Small pool of buyers compared to online Internet marketplaces

Auctions at vertical marketplaces:

As mentioned earlier, vertical marketplaces focus on a particular industry. Sellers doing business on the site tend to be manufacturers or distributors within that industry, while the buyers are distributors or end users of the products. A number of vertical marketplaces now enable sellers to auction their assets, including eSteel.com, Metalsite.com and e-chemicals.com.

There are benefits associated with auctioning your surplus on a vertical site. You are likely to have access to more buyers than if you operated your own company site. And, because of the specialized nature of the site, buyers who visit the site are likely to have an interest in your surplus assets.

However, there are some disadvantages as well. You won't have access to buyers from outside of your narrow industry – so you could be missing out on a number of potential buyers.

EXAMPLE: Jim is the inventory manager for Russell Paints. He is anxious to get rid of 40,000 gallons of surplus paint. Jim decides to list the goods on Paint-site.com, a vertical marketplace. The users of the site who might see Jim's listing include paint distributors, paint retailers and paint liquidators. They are all potential buyers of paint and that's great for Jim.

However, there are also many distributors and liquidators that handle a slightly broader range of goods. Some of them could be interested

buyers, but they are unlikely to see Jim's listing. For example, TX Hardware Liquidation buys and sells surplus paint – and also surplus tools, surplus garden equipment, electrical supplies, nails and screws, etc. Given the range of products it handles, TX simply doesn't have the resources to monitor Paint-site.com or the other vertical sites for all categories of goods it buys. So although TX might have been interested in buying Jim's surplus paint, TX won't learn about the opportunity. That means less competition – and a lower selling price.

Jim's buddy Fred handles surplus equipment disposal for Russell Paints. Fred wants to sell off three old forklifts that the company just replaced with new ones. Jim tells Fred about Paint-site.com, and Fred decides to use the site to sell the forklifts. That's a mistake. Companies in a wide range of industries can utilize a forklift. But companies outside of the paint business won't be logging onto Paint-site.com. So, by listing the forklifts on Paint-site.com, Fred limits his pool of potential buyers – and that will limit the price he realizes from the sale.

Auctions at horizontal marketplaces:

Horizontal marketplace sites enable companies to buy and sell virtually anything, from commodities to factory equipment to finished goods inventory.

Sellers can be manufacturers, service firms, distributors and dealers across all different industries: an equipment dealer selling used processing equipment; an insurance firm selling old office furniture; or a confections company selling surplus candy.

Buyers can include other manufacturers, liquidators, distributors, dealers and exporters. Because there are so many categories of items, horizontal marketplaces will naturally draw the largest pool of potential buyers. That makes horizontal marketplaces an ideal venue for selling your surplus assets – especially via an auction format. That's because the large pool of buyers, in competition with each other, will generate an optimal market price for your assets.

Additional benefits for sellers include the relatively low cost of selling, and the fact that the site itself bears the costs of marketing to drive buyers to the site. And, because horizontal marketplaces enjoy great economies of scale from serving large numbers of buyers and sellers, they can expend the necessary resources to support cutting-edge site functionality and scalability.

E-Commerce

The following chart summarizes the relative benefits of selling your surplus assets on the three types of sites.

	Company Site	Vertical Site	Horizontal Site
Site Development	Very costly	No Cost to Seller	No Cost to Seller
Site Scalability and Functionality	Usually Low	Moderate	High
Sales Commission	None	Modest	Modest
Marketing	Very Costly	No Cost to Seller	No Cost to Seller
Buyer Reach	Narrow	Moderate	Broad
Optimal Pricing	No	No	Yes

TradeOut.com – The Leading Online Marketplace for Business Surplus

- TradeOut.com Overview
- Every Business Can Buy or Sell on TradeOut.com
- Seller Benefits
- Buyer Benefits
- How to Use TradeOut.com
- Tips for Sellers – Creating the Best Opportunity for Selling Your Surplus

TradeOut.com – The Leading Online Marketplace for Business Surplus

A. TradeOut.com Overview

TradeOut.com is the world's leading online surplus marketplace, bringing together buyers and sellers, around the world and across industries, to share information and transact business.

What makes TradeOut.com different from other marketplaces? **TradeOut.com provides online buying and selling, with true e-commerce capability. Sales are done via fixed-price or auction format, and the deal gets done online. There is no need for faxing and phoning. No haggling over terms. And because TradeOut.com matches sellers with the right buyers, sellers get a fair market price for their surplus assets.**

The website is tested and proven, and thousands of businesses already have joined the TradeOut.com community.

B. Every Business Can Buy and Sell on TradeOut.com

SELLERS	BUYERS
Manufacturers and distributors with excess inventory	Discount retailers
Manufacturing firms selling used plant equipment	Manufacturing firms buying equipment
Liquidators, jobbers and closeout dealers	Liquidators, jobbers and closeout dealers
Companies with surplus office equipment	Exporters
Used machinery and equipment dealers	Used machinery and equipment dealers

C. Seller Benefits

According to TradeOut.com research, companies selling surplus assets are primarily interested in four things: (1) true market prices, (2) speed, (3) control and flexibility, and (4) reliability.

TradeOut.com provides all of these benefits ... and many more. Here's how your company can benefit from selling on TradeOut.com:

TradeOut.com

You will generate a true market price on the sale

- You reach a larger pool of buyers – the "right" buyers – to generate true competition.

- The auction format is proven to bring better prices. It allows for concurrent bidding by multiple buyers – compared to the serial negotiations via phone or fax that are typical of traditional selling.

- Bidders are notified when their offers are exceeded, so they can come back with a higher bid if they choose.

CASE STUDY: A large energy company listed 12 diesel generators for auction on TradeOut.com. According to the seller, if he used traditional methods he could expect to sell the generators for $2.4 million, and the process would take 4-5 months. However, on TradeOut.com, the listing was seen by a buyer with whom the seller had not done business before. That buyer offered $2.8 million for the generators, and the transaction was completed in less than 30 days.

You will sell your surplus faster – and generate cash faster

- You can tap into a pool of thousands of buyers, increasing your likelihood of receiving multiple offers right away.

- Terms are set when the sale closes. Lengthy negotiations are a thing of the past.

CASE STUDY: A Midwestern power company was saddled with 40 reels of unneeded fiber optic cable for 2 years, unable to locate any interested buyers.

Yet, less than 2 weeks after listing the cable for sale on TradeOut.com, a buyer from the telecommunications industry purchased all 40 reels for a price in excess of $1 million.

You have flexibility and control

- **Choose the sale format:**

  - First Come First Serve. This is a straight fixed-price sale. It is the fastest way to sell something.

- Standard Auction. This is the ascending auction format with which most people are familiar. You list the assets in a single lot. Buyers make competing bids, and the high bid wins. To protect your interests, you can set a reserve price. If no offer meets the reserve price, you won't have to sell the item.

- Multi-Item Auction. You can sell multiple lots of identical items and buyers can make a bid for one or more of the lots. The winning buyers are those offering the highest bids on a per lot basis, enabling you to maximize your revenue on the auction.

- Charitable Contribution. You indicate the fair market value of the assets and use the site to help find the "right" charitable organization.

• **Choose the sale duration:** 30 days, 6 months ... or something in between. You decide.

• **Control which buyers participate:**

  - In most cases, it is to your advantage to make the item available to all registered users.

  - If you are very concerned about channel conflict, you can restrict the sale to a pre-approved group of buyers. Or you can block out certain buyers selectively. You have the flexibility.

  - Use TradeOut.com as your Intranet to manage intra-company asset transfers. Many large companies have yet to connect all company locations to their Intranet, but virtually all managers have Internet access. TradeOut.com allows you to reach all purchasing managers in your company simultaneously to let them evaluate the available surplus.

• **Choose the terms of sale:**

  - Select the payment terms. You can extend credit or require cash upfront. And you can be paid online, directly through the website.

  - Select the shipping terms for the items.

You can target buyers with precision

- TradeOut.com can instantly notify selected buyers via email when listings are posted. With this capability, TradeOut.com lets you engage in effective one-to-one marketing to drive key buying prospects to your listings.

You can easily track your listings

- You can be notified when new high bids are received on your listed items.

- You can review the current status of listed items at any time.

- You receive notification when sales are closed.

- You can link your own internal inventory management system or ERP system directly to TradeOut.com, allowing for easy item posting and accurate tracking and accounting.

You don't spend valuable time discussing basic information

- You post the item description, photo, blueprints, etc. only once. Buyers get this key information from the site without bothering you. If they have additional questions, they can contact you via email through the site.

- You choose the payment terms and shipping terms. And in a First Come First Serve sale, you also set the price. When a buyer makes an offer on your listing, he or she has agreed to your terms. There is no need for negotiating.

- No more hours spent phoning and faxing back and forth with potential buyers.

CASE STUDY: A leading manufacturer of home fragrance products listed two truckloads of candles and fragrance oils in a Standard Auction on TradeOut.com. While the auction was ongoing, the seller was able to focus on other business matters rather than devoting time to contacting and negotiating with liquidators. When the auction closed, the winning bid exceeded the seller's reserve price and the deal was completed.

You can access all of your records online

- Refer back to what you've sold in the past.

- Check on your current billing status at any time.

- Compare the prices and terms of items you sold with similar items listed by other sellers. That can help guide you in setting prices and terms for future listings.

You don't have to commit big resources to sell on TradeOut.com

- There are no upfront membership fees. Sellers pay a nominal fee of $10 per listing, plus a 5% commission upon completion of the sale. Compare that to the huge cost of setting up your own company-operated site.

- There are no long-term commitments. If you are not satisfied with the selling experience, you don't have to list any additional items for sale.

You can do business whenever and wherever you want to

- TradeOut.com is open for business 24 hours a day, every day of the year.

- The site is accessible globally and in multiple languages.

You can check on the reliability of buyers

- Utilize online D&B summary ratings of companies.

- Review community feedback on the buyer based on his or her previous transactions.

TradeOut.com

- Post your company's credit application on the site to allow buyers to obtain credit approval prior to making an offer on your listing.

You can bank on TradeOut.com's reliability

- TradeOut.com is powered by state-of-the-art, world-class hardware and operating systems. The site architecture has been customized to support critical business functions, provide extensive security and deliver uptime in excess of 99.9%. And the system is supported by an experienced, proven technical team with extensive e-commerce experience.[8]

As a way of summarizing, let's take a look at an example that illustrates the benefits of selling on TradeOut.com:

EXAMPLE: Gunther, the inventory manager at Midwest Power Tools Mfg., has a truckload of surplus drills, routers and saws. The manufacturing cost of the goods is $40,000, and the regular wholesale price is estimated at $100,000.

Traditional Selling

Gunther calls up Bob's Hardware Liquidation, the firm to whom he usually sells his surplus. Since there is no competition, Bob offers Gunther only $25,000.

Gunther decides to find some more liquidators. He contacts two additional closeout dealers that he finds in the yellow pages: ABC General Liquidation and Jim the Jobber. Neither firm regularly handles power tools.

---

[8]Details of the site architecture are as follows: TradeOut.com uses a cutting-edge Oracle database installed on a multi-processor Sun server to manage the growing back-end and data storage requirements, as well as to provide a means of storing and manipulating end-user profiling and preference information. (Oracle is the database in 67% of the top Internet sites.)

TradeOut.com provides web services to the Internet using Compaq ProLiant servers running Microsoft NT, IIS and ASP scripts. A Cisco Local Director balances load, provides fault tolerance and dynamically routes web traffic. Two additional Sun servers provide outbound and corporate email services. The TradeOut.com site is designed with equipment redundancy and fail over in mind to achieve dependable, continuous operations. To provide network security and redundancy, the site's infrastructure is located in a secure data center managed by Exodus Communications, the country's top Internet host provider. Exodus provides extremely reliable, high-speed connectivity to the Internet, certified Microsoft/Oracle/Sun system engineers, extensive site security, redundant power systems, and daily information backups. With the robust architecture and external hosting by Exodus, TradeOut.com has achieved uptime in excess of 99.9% and scalability for unlimited concurrent users.

ABC offers Gunther $30,000, and the following week, after repeated phone calls, Jim the Jobber sends Gunther an offer via fax for $35,000.

Gunther accepts Jim's $35,000 offer. But, Jim now decides that he wants to pay Gunther in 30 days – or else there is no deal. They continue to negotiate for another few days, at which time Gunther reluctantly agrees to Jim's terms.

Summary: It took Gunther five weeks to get the deal done. He estimates that he spent six hours of his time contacting the liquidators and negotiating the deal. In the end, he sold the surplus tools below cost, and accepted payment terms that were less than optimal.

Selling on TradeOut.com

Gunther posts the truckload for sale on TradeOut.com. He selects a Standard Auction, with a 30-day duration. He sets the reserve price at $40,000, and chooses his payment terms – cash upfront.

TradeOut.com immediately sends an email to all registered users interested in hardware items and tools. Four liquidation firms that specialize in that area start bidding actively.

Each time there is a new high bid, TradeOut.com sends Gunther a brief email message that lets him track the progress of the auction.

When the auction closes, the winning bid is $55,000. TradeOut.com notifies Gunther and the winning bidder via email, and they get in touch to arrange for the transfer of the truckload.

Summary: Gunther spent two minutes to register on TradeOut.com, plus five minutes to post the item and ten minutes monitoring the sale. And, because he was able to reach more of the right buyers via the online auction, he made a profit on the sale.

TRADITIONAL SELLING

Cost of Goods	($40,000)
Value of Gunther's time spent selling the tools (6 hours @ 150/hr)	($900)
Revenue from Sale	$35,000
Profit/(Loss)	($5,900)

SELLING ON TRADEOUT.COM

Cost of Goods	($40,000)
Value of Gunther's time spent selling the tools (17 min. @ 150/hr)	($42)
Revenue from Sale	$55,000
Profit/(Loss)	$14,958

TradeOut.com

D. Buyer Benefits

TradeOut.com also provides tremendous benefits for companies seeking to buy surplus. Here's how you can benefit as a buyer.

You get access to more surplus assets

- Sellers from around the world are listing their surplus on TradeOut.com. You'll find more of the kinds of items you are interested in buying.

- You can browse and buy many categories of items. TradeOut.com is a true horizontal marketplace, providing buying opportunities in more than 100 categories of finished goods, operating assets and excess capacity.

- Because sellers are able to target interested buyers, buyers can benefit as well. During registration, you select the categories of surplus in which you are most interested. TradeOut.com will send you instant email notification when any such items are listed for sale. This allows TradeOut.com to match the right buyers and sellers.

You can buy what you want more quickly

- TradeOut.com shortens the buying and selling cycle. Selling terms are already set. If you see an item you want in a First Come First Serve sale, and you agree to the seller's terms, just place the offer and it's yours. No need to negotiate. You can have the item in your hands quickly.

- In an auction format, the item gets sold to the high bidder. No haggling. No negotiating. No wasting time.

You can search quickly

- No more searching for surplus goods in classified ads and catalog listings. TradeOut.com allows for easy searching – by category, by seller or by keyword. It takes just seconds to search.

- Create a custom profile. Each time you log in, TradeOut.com will automatically search for your preferred items.

- Look at selling prices for comparable items that are currently listed or which sold previously, as an indicator of how much you might need to offer.

You can get additional information

- Though most item listings will have full descriptions, you may still have additional questions that you want to ask the seller. Or you may want to arrange a site visit to inspect the items. TradeOut.com allows for email communication through the site.

- Check out the reliability of the seller using online D&B summary ratings and TradeOut.com community feedback.

You don't have to monitor the auction constantly

- Automatic bidding allows you to put in a maximum bid that you are willing to pay for an item. TradeOut.com then bids for you whenever another buyer exceeds your bid, up to your maximum.

You can use TradeOut.com anytime

- TradeOut.com never closes. 24 hour/7day access allows you to conduct business on the site after normal hours if you desire. Place new offers anytime. Track the status of your existing offers anytime.

You can use TradeOut.com for reselling

- Many companies buy and sell on TradeOut.com. You can use TradeOut.com to resell an item that you bought on the site.

You can link to logistics providers

- TradeOut.com has established direct online links to companies that can handle your payment, shipping and insurance needs.

Here's an example that illustrates the benefits of buying on TradeOut.com:

EXAMPLE: *Buzz Masters owns and operates a lumber mill in Spokane. His main saw is 12 years old and has been breaking down too often. It's time to replace it, but Buzz is a little light on cash. He decides to look for used equipment.*

Traditional Buying

Buzz knows of several dealers that specialize in used milling equipment. But he knows they'll have a high asking price. So Buzz decides to do the legwork and contact other lumber mills directly.

Buzz takes out an industry directory and starts dialing. He speaks to some people and leaves many messages – but no one has what he is looking for. After three weeks, time is running out because the current saw is on its last legs.

So Buzz turns to the used equipment dealers. He contacts six dealers located in the Northwest and he finds a dealer in Oregon who has the right kind of saw. The dealer is asking $1.1 million.

Buzz travels to Oregon to inspect the equipment and see the maintenance records. Everything looks okay. He tries, unsuccessfully, to negotiate the price down, and then agrees to pay the $1.1 million.

Summary: It took Buzz almost six weeks to acquire the equipment. He estimates that he spent 40 hours of his time contacting the other lumber mills and another 4 hours negotiating with the used equipment dealer in Oregon. In the end, he got what he wanted, but it took six weeks and he paid top dollar.

Buying on TradeOut.com

Buzz goes to TradeOut.com and looks at the Forestry/Logging/Lumber Equipment category. He doesn't see exactly what he wants. But he takes two minutes to register and fill out his category preferences.

Three days later, Jones, a mill owner in Michigan, lists a saw on TradeOut.com. He's asking $900,000 in a First Come First Serve sale.

Because Buzz indicated an interest in Lumber equipment when he registered, TradeOut.com immediately notifies Buzz of Jones' new listing via email. Buzz reviews the photos of the equipment and the detailed specs that Jones posted on the website. He sends Jones a couple of questions via email, and gets back a prompt response.

Even with the $15,000 it will cost to ship the saw and insure it during transport, Buzz will save close to $200,000 if he buys the saw on TradeOut.com vs. buying a saw from a dealer. Buzz logs onto TradeOut.com and places the offer for $900,000. At that point, the sale is closed.

__Summary__: Buzz spent a total of 30 minutes reviewing the listing and corresponding with the seller. TradeOut.com was able to match the right buyer and seller through targeted marketing. Buzz got a great deal, and he had the equipment in his possession within a couple of weeks.

E. How to Use TradeOut.com

Buying and selling on TradeOut.com is very simple. The website is easy-to-use, enabling buyers and sellers to transact business without the need for active involvement from TradeOut.com. (However, TradeOut.com customer service is available to assist any users who require help. Just call 888-525-TRADE.)

You don't need to be registered to browse the site, but you do have to register to buy or sell. Registration is free.

- **Registration (approximate time 2 minutes)**
- **Selling Steps (approximate time 3-5 minutes)**
    1. Click on "Seller Services", and then click "Posting an Item"
    2. Fill in all of the fields
        - category
        - item title
        - quantity
        - type of sale
        - reserve price or fixed selling price
        - payment and shipping terms
        - item location
        - detailed description (if applicable)
    3. Review the listing for accuracy
    4. Approve for posting
- **Buying Steps (as little as 1 or 2 minutes)**
    1. Review item listings
    2. Make an offer

TradeOut.com

When the sale or auction closes, TradeOut.com will send an email to the seller and the winning buyer. At that point, the parties contact each other and arrange for payment and physical transfer of the item.

The TradeOut.com website also contains detailed answers to frequently asked questions about the buying and selling process. Click the "Help" button on the website to access this information.

F. Tips for Sellers – Creating the Best Opportunity for Selling Your Surplus

For a product to sell at retail, it has to get the buyer's attention, it has to look good, it should convey quality, it must be priced reasonably, and it should make the buyer feel confident about his or her purchase.

The same guidelines apply to selling on TradeOut.com. To help ensure that your listing will attract offers, we suggest that you follow as many of these guidelines as possible:

"Title" • Carefully word your **item title.** These few words are all that most buyers will see as they browse the site. If your title is vague or poorly written, buyers may not be inclined to click on the listing for more details. Conversely, if the item title is clearly written and contains adequate information, you should generate more buyer interest.

 • Add **photos** to your listings. A picture is truly worth a thousand words. Instructions for including a photo with your listing are contained on the site.

 • Provide as much **detail** as possible. Place yourself in the shoes of a potential buyer. What information would you want to know? Include all of that … and then some. It makes your item more salable, and also shows that you have nothing to hide.

 • Provide a reasonable **warranty** if you are able. It reduces buyer risk and should increase the selling price.

• Be completely honest about the **condition** of the asset. If you misrepresent, the buyer will eventually determine the truth and the deal will become undone. That wastes everyone's time, including yours.

- Offer to provide **maintenance records** when selling used equipment.

- **Identify** your company. Although TradeOut.com does enable you to post items for sale and withhold your company name from the listing, you should do so only in exceptional circumstances. Disclosing who you are enhances the credibility and appeal of the listing, especially if your company is well-known.

- Choose your selling **category** very carefully. For example, if your company is in the printing industry and you are selling a press, it is obvious that the item should be listed under the Printing equipment category. However, if you are also selling a forklift that your company uses to move rolls of paper, you should think twice before listing it under Printing equipment. That forklift can be used in many industries, and a better place to list it would be the Material Handling equipment category. The same logic would apply for a compressor (Compressor category) or a motor (Electrical/Power/Motors category).

  As a general rule, if the equipment or machinery can be used in multiple industries, you probably should list it in one of the categories under General Commercial Equipment. If the equipment is unique to your industry, it probably belongs in one of the categories under Industry-Specific Equipment. Posting items for sale in the proper category will give you access to more interested buyers, which should help generate betters selling prices for your surplus assets. (If you have any uncertainty about where to list an item, contact a TradeOut.com salesperson or TradeOut.com customer service.)

- Allow potential buyers to **contact** you with questions. The posting form enables you to choose whether or not prospective buyers may contact you via email. If you don't make yourself available to respond to inquiries, you may sharply limit the number of offers you will receive on the item – especially high-priced items or items of a technical nature.

- Bring your **previous buyers** to the site. If the buyers to whom you have previously sold surplus items participate in your TradeOut.com auctions, you will increase the pool of buyers for your items and generate more competition. Therefore, encourage those buyers to register on the site so that TradeOut.com can send them email notification of your listings. Also, you should provide TradeOut.com with the names of other potential buyers of your surplus, which will enable TradeOut.com to contact them about registering.

- Be realistic in setting your **prices**. If you seek more than the item is reasonably worth, there's a good chance you won't conclude the sale. You can always repost the goods at a lower price if they don't sell at the higher price, but by then you may have wasted weeks. And time is money as we've seen. In most cases, it's preferable to realize a reasonable sum of money for your surplus the first time around than not sell it at all. In an auction format, set your **reserve price** as low as you can. Then watch competitive forces bid up the price.

To recap:

- Carefully word your item title

- Use photos

- Provide details

- Provide a warranty

- Disclose the true condition

- Provide maintenance records

- Identify your company

- Choose your category carefully

- Allow buyers to contact you

- Bring your existing buyers to the site

- Set realistic prices

If you follow this checklist each time you post a new listing, chances are you will realize a much higher selling price for your surplus assets.

Appendix A – Directory of Key Trade and Professional Associations

Agriculture

Agriculture Council of America
11020 King St., Suite 205
Overland Park, KS 66210
Phone: 913-491-1895
Fax: 913-491-6502
Website: www.nana.org
President and CEO
– Eldon White

Farm Equipment Manufacturers Ass'n
1000 Executive Parkway
Suite 100
St. Louis, MO 63141
Phone: 314-878-2304
Fax: 314-878-1742
Email: FEMA@aol.com
Website: www.farmequip.org
Executive V. President
– Robert K. Schnell

Nat'l Grain and Feed Ass'n
1201 New York Ave., N.W.
Suite 830
Washington, DC 20005-3917
Phone: 202-289-0873
Fax: 202-289-5388
Website: www.ngfa.org
President – Kendell Keith

Aluminum

Aluminum Ass'n
900 19th St., N.W., Suite 300
Washington, DC 20006
Phone: 202-862-5100
Fax: 202-862-5164
Website: www.aluminum.org
President – J. Stephen Larkin

Aluminum Extruders Council
1000 N. Rand Road, Suite 214
Wauconda, IL 60084
Phone: 847-526-2010
Fax: 847-526-3993
Website: www.aec.org
President
– Donn W. Sanford, CAE

Apparel and Textiles

American Apparel Manufacturers Ass'n
2500 Wilson Blvd., Suite 301
Arlington, VA 22201
Phone: 703-524-1864
Fax: 703-522-6741
Website:
www.americanapparel.org
President – Larry Martin

American Textile Manufacturers Institute
1130 Connecticut Ave, N.W.
Suite 1200
Washington, DC 20036
Phone: 202-862-0500
Fax: 202-862-0570
Website: www.atmi.org
Executive Vice President
– Carlos F.J. Moore

Textile Distributors Ass'n
104 W. 40th St., 18th floor
New York, NY 10018
Phone: 212-869-6300
Fax: 212-869-2346
Exec. Director – Bruce Roberts

Textile Rental Services Ass'n of America
P.O. Box 1283
1130 E. Beach Blvd.
Hallandale, FL 33008-1283
Phone: 954-457-7555
Fax: 954-457-3890
Website: www.trsa.org
Exec. Director – John Contney, CAE

Aviation/Aerospace

Aerospace Industries Association of America
1250 I St. N.W., Suite 1200
Washington, DC 20005-3924
Phone: 202-371-8400
Fax: 202-371-8470
Email: aia@aia-aerospace.org
Website: www.aia-aerospace.org
President – John W. Douglass

Air Transport Ass'n of America
1301 Pennsylvania Ave., N.W.
Suite 1100
Washington, DC 20004-1707
Phone: 202-626-4000
Fax: 202-626-4181
Website: www.air-transport.org
President and CEO
– Carol B. Hallett

Aviation Distributors and Manufacturers Ass'n Int'l
1900 Arch St.
Philadelphia, PA 19103-1498
Phone: 215-564-3484
Fax: 215-564-2175
Executive Director
– Patricia A. Lilly

General Aviation Manufacturers Ass'n
1400 K St., N.W., Suite 801
Washington, DC 20005
Phone: 202-393-1500
Fax: 202-842-4063
President – Edward M. Bolen

Nat'l Air Transportation Ass'n
4226 King St.
Alexandria, VA 22302
Phone: 703-845-9000
Fax: 703-845-8176
Website: www.nata.online.org
President – James K. Coyne

Building Materials

American Architectural Manufacturers Ass'n
1827 Walden Office Sq.
Suite 104
Schaumburg, IL 60173-4268
Phone: 847-303-5664
Fax: 847-303-5774
Executive Director
– Stephen K. Sullivan

American Supply Ass'n
222 Merchandise Mart Plaza
Suite 1360
Chicago, IL 60654-1202
Phone: 312-464-0090
Fax: 312-464-0091
Email: asaemail@interserv.com
Website: www.asa.net
Exec. Director
– Maurice A. Desmarais,
CAE

Ass'n of the Wall and Ceiling Industries-Internat'l
803 W. Broad St., Suite 600
Falls Church, VA 22046-3108
Phone: 703-534-8300
Fax: 703-534-8307
Email: info@awci.org
Website: www.awci.org
Exec. V. President
– Steven A. Etkin, CAE

Door and Hardware Institute
14170 Newbrook Drive
Chantilly, VA 20151-2232
Phone: 703-222-2010
Fax: 703-222-2410
Website: www.dhi.org
Exec. Director – Jerry Heppes, CAE

**Kitchen Cabinet
Manufacturers Ass'n**
1899 Preston White Dr.
Reston, VA 20191-5435
Phone: 703-264-1690
Fax: 703-620-6530
Email: dtitus@kcma.org
Website: www.kcma.org
Exec. V. President
  – C. Richard Titus

**Nat'l Ass'n of Floor Covering
Distributors**
401 N. Michigan Ave.
Chicago IL 60611-4703
Phone: 312-644-6610
Fax: 312-245-1085
Website: www.nafcd.org
Exec. Director
  – Mariann Gregory

Nat'l Concrete Masonry Ass'n
2302 Horse Pen Rd.
Herndon, VA 20171
Phone: 703-713-1900
Fax: 703-713-1910
Email: ncma@ncma.org
Website: www.ncma.org
President – Mark Hogan

Nat'l Kitchen and Bath Ass'n
687 Willow Grove St.
Hackettstown, NJ 07840
Phone: 908-852-0033
Fax: 908-852-1695
COO – Cecelia Balazs

Nat'l Paint and Coatings Ass'n
1500 Rhode Island Ave., N.W.
Washington, DC 20005-5503
Phone: 202-462-6272
202-462-8549
President – J. Andrew Doyle

**Nat'l Wood Window
and Door Ass'n**
1400 East Touhy Ave.
Suite 470
Des Plaines, IL 60018-3305
Phone: 847-299-5200
Fax: 847-299-1286
Website: www.nwwda.org
President – Alan Campbell, CAE

**North American Building
Material Distribution Ass'n**
401 N. Michigan Ave.
Chicago, IL 60611-4274
Phone: 312-321-6845
Fax: 312-644-0310
Email: nbmda@sba.com
Website: www.nbmda.org
Exec. V. President
  – Kevin Gammonley

Wallcoverings Ass'n
401 N. Michigan Ave.
Chicago, IL 60611-4267
Phone: 312-644-6610
Fax: 312-527-6774
Exec. Director – Ron Pietrzak

Carriers

American Trucking Ass'ns
2200 Mill Road
Alexandria, VA 22314-4677
Phone: 703-838-1700
Fax: 703-684-5751
Website: www.trucking.org
President and CEO
  – Walter B. McCormick, Jr.

**Intermodal Ass'n of North
America**
7501 Greenway Center Dr.
Suite 720
Greenbelt, MD 20770
Phone: 301-982-3400
Fax: 301-982-4815
Email: iana@intermodal.org
Website: www.intermodal.org
President – Joanne Casey

Chemicals

**Chemical Manufacturers
Association**
1300 Wilson Blvd.
Arlington, VA 22209-2307
Phone: 703-741-5000
Fax: 703-741-6000
Website: www.cmahq.com
President & CEO
  – Frederick Webber

Computers/Information
Technology

**Information Technology Ass'n
of America**
1616 N. Ft. Myer Dr.
Suite 1300
Arlington, VA 22209-3106
Phone: 703-522-5055
Fax: 703-525-2279
Email: hmiller@itaa.org
Website: www.ITAA.org
President – Harris Miller

**Information Technology
Industry Council**
1250 I St., N.W., Suite 200
Washington, DC 20005-3922
Phone: 202-737-8888
Fax: 202-638-4922
Website: www.itic.org
President – Rhett Dawson

**Semiconductor Equipment
and Materials Internat'l**
805 E. Middlefield Rd.
Mountain View, CA 94043-4080
Phone: 650-940-6911
Fax: 650-967-5375
Website: www.semi.org
President – Stanley Myers

Semiconductor Industry Ass'n
181 Metro Drive, Suite 450
San Jose, CA 95110
Phone: 408-436-6600
Fax: 408-436-6646
Website: www.semichips.org
President – George Scalise

Construction

**American Road and
Transportation Builders
Assocation**
1010 Massachusetts Ave., N.W.
Washington, DC 20001
Phone: 202-289-4434
Fax: 202-289-4435
Website: www.artba-hq.org
President and CEO
  – T. Peter Ruane, CAE

**Associated Builders and
Contractors**
1300 North 17th St., Suite 800
Rosslyn, VA 22209
Phone: 703-812-2000
Fax: 703-812-8200
Website: www.abc.org
Executive Vice President
  – Robert Hepner

**Associated Equipment
Distributors**
615 West 22nd St.
Oak Brook, IL 60523
Phone: 630-574-0650
Fax: 630-574-0132
Email: jtm@macknet.com
Website: www.aednet.org
Exec. V. President – Toby Mack

**Construction Industry
Manufacturers Ass'n**
111 E. Wisconsin Ave.
Suite 1000
Milwaukee, WI 53202-4879
Phone: 414-272-0943
Fax: 414-272-1170
Email: cima@cimanet.com
Website: www.cimanet.com
Exec. V.P. and COO
  – Dennis Slater

Consumer Packaged Goods

Grocery Manufacturers of America
1010 Wisconsin Ave., N.W.
Suite 900
Washington, DC 20007-3694
Phone: 202-337-9400
Fax: 202-337-4508
Email: webmaster@gmabrands.com
Website: www.gmabrands.com
President – C. Manly Molpus

Educational Products

Educational Dealers and Suppliers Ass'n Internat'l
711 West 17th St., Suite J-5
Costa Mesa, CA 92627
Phone: 714-642-3986
Fax: 714-642-7960
Email: edsaintl@aol.com
Director – Allen Warren

Nat'l School Supply and Equipment Ass'n
8300 Colesville Road, Suite 250
Silver Spring, MD 20910
Phone: 301-495-0240
Fax: 301-495-3330
Email: nssea@nssea.org
Website: www.nssea.org
President – Tim Holt

Electrical/Electronics

Consumer Electronics Manufacturers Association
2500 Wilson Blvd.
Arlington, VA 22201
Phone: 703-907-7600
Fax: 703-907-7692
Website: www.cemacity.org
President – Gary J. Shapiro

Electronic Industries Ass'n
2500 Wilson Blvd.
Arlington, VA 22201
Phone: 703-907-7500
Fax: 703-907-7501
Website: www.eia.org
President – David McCurdy, CAE

Nat'l Ass'n of Electrical Distributors
1100 Corporate Square Drive
Suite 100
St. Louis, MO 63132
Phone: 314-991-9000
Fax: 314-991-3060
Email: info@naed.org
Website: www.naed.org
President – Joel Hoiland, CAE

Nat'l Electrical Manufacturers Ass'n
1300 N. 17th St., Suite 1847
Rosslyn, VA 22209
Phone: 703-841-3200
Fax: 703-841-3351
Email: webmaster@nema.org
Website: www.nema.org
President
– Malcolm O'Hagan, Ph.D.

Nat'l Electronic Distributors Ass'n
1111 Alderman Dr., Suite 400
Alpharetta, GA 30005-4143
Phone: 678-393-9990
Fax: 678-393-9998
Website: www.nedassoc.org
Exec. V. President – Robin Gray, Jr.

Export Firms

American Ass'n of Exporters and Importers
11 W. 42nd St., 30th Floor
New York, NY 10036
Phone: 212-944-2230
Fax: 212-382-2606
President – Eugene J. Milosh

Nat'l Ass'n of Export Companies
P.O. Box 1330
Murray Hill Station
New York, NY 10156
Phone: 212-490-7966
Fax: 718-596-5111
Website: www.nexco.org
Exec. Director – Nina Liebman

Food and Beverages

American Institute of Food Distribution
28-12 Broadway
Fair Lawn, NJ 07410-3913
Phone: 201-791-5570
Fax: 201-791-5222
Email: rpfaff@foodinstitute.com
Website: www.foodinstitute.com
President – Rick Pfaff

Beer Institute
122 C. St., N.W., Suite 750
Washington, DC 20001
Phone: 202-737-2337
Fax: 202-737-7004
Website: www.beerinst.org
President – Raymond McGrath

Biscuit and Cracker Manufacturers Ass'n
8484 Georgia Ave., Suite 700
Silver Spring, MD 20910-5604
Phone: 301-608-1552
Fax: 301-608-1557
Website: www.thebcma.org
President – Francis P. Rooney

Can Manufacturers Institute
1625 Massachusetts Ave., N.W.
Suite 500
Washington, DC 20036-2212
Phone: 202-232-4677
Fax: 202-232-5756
Website: www.cancentral.com
President – Robert Budway

Flavor and Extract Manufacturers Ass'n of the United States
1620 I St., N.W., Suite 925
Washington, DC 20006
Phone: 202-293-5800
Fax: 202-463-8998
Attorney and Exec. Secretary
– Daniel Thompson

Food Distributors Internat'l
201 Park Washington Court
Falls Church, VA 22046-4521
Phone: 703-532-9400
Fax: 703-538-4173
President – John Block

Food Marketing Institute
800 Connecticut Ave., N.W.
Suite 500
Washington, DC 20006-2701
Phone: 202-452-8444
Fax: 202-429-4519
Email: fmi@fmi.org
Website: www.fmi.org
President and CEO
– Timothy Hammonds

Food Processing Machinery and Supplies Ass'n
200 Daingerfield Rd.
Alexandria, VA 22314-2884
Phone: 703-684-1080
Fax: 703-548-6563
Email: fpmsa@clark.net
Website: www.fpmsa.org
President and CEO
– George Melnykovich, Ph.D.

**Foodservice Equipment
Distributors Ass'n**
223 W. Jackson Blvd., Suite 620
Chicago, IL 60606
Phone: 312-427-9605
Fax: 312-427-9607
Website: www.cfeda.com
Exec. Director
    – Raymond Herrick, II, CAE

**Internat'l Ass'n of Food
Industry Suppliers**
1451 Dolly Madison Blvd.
McLean, VA 22101-3850
Phone: 703-761-2600
Fax: 703-761-4334
Email: info@iafis.org
Website: www.iafis.org
President – Charles W. Bray

**Internat'l Foodservice
Manufacturers Ass'n**
180 N. Stetson Ave., Suite 4400
Chicago, IL 60601
Phone: 312-540-4400
Fax: 312-540-4401
Website:
www.foodserviceworld.com/ifma
President – Michael Licata

**Nat'l Confectioners Ass'n of
the United States**
7900 Westpark Dr., Suite A320
McLean, VA 22102-4203
Phone: 703-790-5750
Fax: 703-790-5752
Website: www.candyusa.org
President – Lawrence Graham

**Nat'l Council of Chain
Restaurants**
325 7th St., N.W., Suite 1000
Washington, DC 20004
Phone: 202-626-8183
Fax: 202-626-8185
Exec. Director – Terrie Dort

Nat'l Food Distributors Ass'n
401 N. Michigan Ave.
Chicago, IL 60611-4267
Phone: 312-644-6610
Fax: 312-321-6869
Managing Director
    – Arthur Klawans

Nat'l Food Processors Ass'n
1350 I St., N.W., Suite 300
Washington, DC 20005
Phone: 202-639-5963
Fax: 202-637-8464
President and CEO – John Cady

Nat'l Soft Drink Ass'n
1101 16th St., N.W.
Washington, DC 20036-4803
Phone: 202-463-6732
Fax: 202-463-8172
Website: www.nsda.org
President – William L. Ball, III

**North American Ass'n of Food
Equipment Manufacturers**
401 N. Michigan Ave.
Chicago, IL 60611-4267
Phone: 312-644-6610
Fax: 312-527-6658
Email: nafem_hq@sba.com
Website: www.nafem.org
Exec. V. President
    – Maxine Lee Couture

Snack Food Ass'n
1711 King St., Suite 1
Alexandria, VA 22314-2720
Phone: 703-836-4500
Fax: 703-836-8262
Email: sfa@sfa.org
Website: www.snax.com
President – James Shufelt

Footwear

Athletic Footwear Ass'n
200 Castlewood Dr.
N. Palm Beach, FL 33408
Phone: 561-842-4100
Fax: 561-863-8984
Email: jhsgma@aol.com
Website: www.sportlink.com
Exec. Director – Gregg Hartley

**Footwear Industries of
America**
1420 K St., N.W., Suite 600
Washington, DC 20005
Phone: 202-789-1420
Fax: 202-789-4058
Email: fawn@fia.org
Website: www.fia.org
President – Fawn Evenson

Furniture/Home
Furnishings

**American Furniture
Manufacturers Ass'n**
P.O. Box HP-7
High Point, NC 27261
Phone: 910-884-5000
Fax: 910-884-5303
Exec. V. President
    – Douglas L. Brackett

American Lighting Ass'n
2050 Stemmons Freeway
Suite 10046
P.O. Box 420288
Dallas, TX 75342-0288
Phone: 214-698-9898
Fax: 214-698-9899
Website:
www.americanlightingassoc.com
President – Richard D. Upton

**Internat'l Furniture Rental
Ass'n**
9202 N. Meridian St., Suite 200
Indianapolis, IN 46260
Phone: 317-571-5613
Fax: 317-571-5603
Exec. Director
    – Jerry Gorup, CAE

Internat'l Sleep Products Ass'n
333 Commerce St.
Alexandria, VA 22314
Phone: 703-683-8371
Fax: 703-683-4503
Website: www.sleepproducts.org
Exec. V. President
    – Russell L. Abolt

**Juvenile Products
Manufacturers Ass'n**
236 Rte. 38 West, Suite 100
Moorestown, NJ 08057
Phone: 609-231-8500
Fax: 609-231-4664
Email: jpma@ahint.com
Website: www.jpma.com
Exec. V. President
    – Robert Waller, Jr.

Garden Equipment

**Lawn and Garden Marketing
and Distribution Ass'n**
1900 Arch St.
Philadelphia, PA 19103-1498
Phone: 215-564-3484
Fax: 215-564-2175
Email: assnhqt@netaxs.com
Website: www.lgmda.org
Exec. Director
    – John McGreevey, Jr.

**Outdoor Power Equipment
Institute**
341 South Patrick St.
Alexandria, VA 22314
Phone: 703-549-7600
Fax: 703-549-7604
Email: opeimow@aol.com
Website: www.opei.mow.org
President – Dennis Dix, CAE

Hardware

American Hardware Manufacturers Ass'n
801 N. Plaza Dr.
Schaumburg, IL 60173-4977
Phone: 847-605-1025
Fax: 847-605-1093
Website: www.ahma.org
President and CEO
– William Farrell

Internat'l Hardware Distributors Ass'n
401 N. Michigan Ave.
Suite 2200
Chicago, IL 60611-4267
Phone: 312-644-6610
Fax: 312-527-6640
Email: IHDA@SBA.COM
Managing Director
– Glen Anderson

Health and Beauty

Beauty and Barber Supply Institute
11811 N. Tatum Blvd.
Suite 1085
Phoenix, AZ 85028-1625
Phone: 602-404-1800
Fax: 602-404-8900
Email: spano@bbsi.org
Website: www.bbsi.org
Exec. Director – Michael Spano

Cosmetic, Toiletry and Fragrance Ass'n
1101 17th St., N.W., Suite 300
Washington, DC 20036-4702
Phone: 202-331-1770
Fax: 202-331-1969
Email: www.ctfa.org
President
– E. Edward Kavanaugh

Healthcare

Ass'n for Healthcare Resource Materials and Management
One N. Franklin, 30th Floor
Chicago, IL 60606-3420
Phone: 312-422-3840
Fax: 312-422-4573
Website: www.ahrmm.org
Exec. Director – Albert Sunseri

Health Industry Distributors Ass'n
66 Canal Center Plaza
Suite 520
Alexandria, VA 22314-1591
Phone: 703-549-4432
Fax: 703-549-6495
President and CEO
– S. Wayne Kay

Health Industry Manufacturers Ass'n
1200 G St., N.W., Suite 400
Washington, DC 20005-3814
Phone: 202-783-8700
Fax: 202-783-8750
Website: www.himanet.com
President – Alan Magazine

Heating/Ventilation/Air Conditioning

Air Movement and Control Ass'n Internat'l
30 W. University Drive
Arlington Heights, IL 60004-1893
Phone: 847-394-0150
Fax: 847-253-0088
Email: amca@amca.org
Website: www.amca.org
Exec. V. President
– Peter Hanly

Air-Conditioning and Refrigeration Institute
4301 N. Fairfax Drive
Suite 425
Arlington, VA 22203
Phone: 703-524-8800
Fax: 703-528-3816
Email: ari@ari.org
Website: www.ari.org
President – Clifford H. Rees, Jr.

Northamerican Heating, Refrig. and Air Conditioning Wholesalers Ass'n
P.O. Box 16790
Columbus, OH 43216
Phone: 614-488-1835
Fax: 614-488-0482
Website: www.nhraw.org
Exec. V. President
– James Wilder

Home Appliances

Ass'n of Home Appliance Manufacturers
20 N. Wacker Dr., Suite 1231
Chicago, IL 60606
Phone: 312-984-5800
Fax: 312-984-5823
Email: ahamdc@aol.com
Website: www.aham.org
President – Joseph McGuire

Nat'l Appliance Parts Suppliers Ass'n
16420 S.E. Mcgillivray Blvd.
Suite 103-133
Vancouver, WA 98683
Phone: 360-834-3805
Fax: 360-834-3507
Website:
www.napsa.repairnet.com
Exec. Director – Suzanne Stilwill

Industrial Equipment

American Boiler Manufacturers Association
950 N. Glebe Rd., Suite 160
Arlington, VA 22203-1824
Phone: 703-522-7350
Fax: 703-522-2665
Email: abma@abma.com
Website: www.abma.com
President – Russell Mosher

Electrical Apparatus Service Ass'n
1331 Baur Blvd.
St. Louis, MO 63132
Phone: 314-993-2220
Fax: 314-993-1269
Email: lraynes@easa.com
Website: www.easa.com
Exec. V. President
– Linda Raynes

Equipment Leasing Ass'n of America
4301-N Fairfax Drive, Suite 550
Arlington, VA 22203-1608
Phone: 703-527-8655
Fax: 703-522-7099
Website: www.elaonline.com
President
– Michael Fleming, CAE

Equipment Manufacturers Institute
10 S. Riverside Plaza
Suite 1220
Chicago, IL 60606-3710
Phone: 312-321-1470
Fax: 312-321-1480
Email: emi@emi.org
Website: www.emi.org
President – Emmett Barker

Machinery Dealers Nat'l Ass'n
315 S. Patrick St.
Alexandria, VA 22314-3501
Phone: 703-836-9300
Fax: 703-836-9303
Email: office@mdna.org
Website: www.mdna.org
Executive V. President
– Darryl D. McEwen

Nat'l Welding Supply Ass'n
1900 Arch St.
Philadelphia, PA 19103-1498
Phone: 215-564-3484
Fax: 215-564-2175
Email: nwsa@nwsa.com
Website: www.nwsa.com
Exec. Director – John Derrickson

Production Equipment Rental Ass'n
P.O. Box 55515
Sherman Oaks, CA 91413-0515
Phone: 818-906-2467
Fax: 818-906-1720
Email: peraman@aol.com
Website:
www.productionequipment.com
Exec. Director – Edwin Clare

United Ass'n of Equipment Leasing
520 Third St., Suite 201
Oakland, CA 94607-3520
Phone: 510-444-9235
Fax: 510-444-1346
Exec. V. President
    – Raymond Williams, Ph.D., CAE

Valve Manufacturers Ass'n of America
1050 17th St., N.W., Suite 280
Washington, DC 20036-5503
Phone: 202-331-8105
Fax: 202-296-0378
President
    – William S. Sandler, CAE

Industrial Parts and Supplies

American Gear Manufacturers Ass'n
1500 King St., Suite 201
Alexandria, VA 22314-2730
Phone: 703-684-0211
Fax: 703-684-0242
Email: webmaster@agma.org
President
    – Joe T. Franklin, Jr., CAE

Independent Lubricant Manufacturers Ass'n
651 S. Washington St.
Alexandria, VA 22314
Phone: 703-684-5574
Fax: 703-836-8503
Email: ilma@ilma.org
Website: www.ilma.org
Exec. Director – Richard Ekfelt

Industrial Fasteners Institute
1717 East 9th St., Suite 1105
Cleveland, OH 44114
Phone: 216-241-1482
Fax: 216-241-5901
Email: indfast@aol.com
Website:
www.industrial-fasteners.org
Managing Director
    – Robert Harris

Wire Ass'n Internat'l
1570 Boston Post Rd., Box 578
Guilford, CT 06437-0578
Phone: 203-453-2777
Fax: 203-453-8384
Website: www.wirenet.org
Exec. Director – Paul Casteran

Institutional Supplies

Internat'l Sanitary Supply Ass'n
7373 North Lincoln Ave.
Lincolnwood, IL 60646-1799
Phone: 847-982-0800
Fax: 847-982-1012
Email: issa@info.com
Website: www.ISSA.com
Exec. Director – John Garfinkel

Leasing and Rental

American Rental Ass'n
1900 19th St.
Moline, IL 61265-4198
Phone: 309-764-2475
Fax: 309-764-2747
Website: www.ararental.org
Executive VP – James R. Irish

Ass'n of Progressive Rental Organizations
9015 Mountain Ridge Dr.
Suite 220
Austin, TX 78759-7252
Phone: 512-794-0095
Fax: 512-794-0097
Website: www.apro/rto.com
Executive Director – Bill Keese

Logistics

Internat'l Warehouse Logistics Ass'n
1300 West Higgins Rd.
Suite 111
Park Ridge, IL 60068-5764
Phone: 847-292-1891
Fax: 847-292-1896
Email: logistx@aol.com
Website:
www.warehouselogistics.org
President – Michael Jenkins

Manufacturing

National Association of Manufacturers
1331 Pennsylvania Ave., N.W.
Suite 600
Washington, DC 20004-1790
Phone: 202-637-3087
Fax: 202-637-3182
Email: manufacturing@nam.org
Website: www.nam.org
President – Jerry Jasinowski

Marine

Nat'l Ass'n of Marine Products and Services
200 E. Randolph Drive
Suite 5100
Chicago, IL 60601
Phone: 312-946-6200
Fax: 312-946-6263
Contact – Tammy Rossow

Nat'l Marine Manufacturers Ass'n
200 E. Randolph Drive
Suite 5100
Chicago, IL 60601-6436
Phone: 312-946-6200
Fax: 312-946-0388
President – Jeffrey W. Napier

Shipbuilders Council of America
1600 Wilson Blvd., Suite 1000
Arlington, VA 22209
Phone: 703-351-6734
President – Allen Walker

Material Handling

Material Handling Equipment Distributors Ass'n
201 U.S. Hwy. 45
Vernon Hills, IL 60061-2398
Phone: 847-680-3500
Fax: 847-362-6989
Email: connect@mheda.org
Website: www.mheda.org
Exec. V. President – Liz Richards

Material Handling Industry Ass'n
8720 Red Oak Blvd., Suite 201
Charlotte, NC 28217-3957
Phone: 704-676-1190
Fax: 704-676-1199
Website: www.mhia.org
CEO – Albert Leffler

Media/Entertainment/ Publishing

Ass'n of American Publishers
1718 Connecticut Ave., N.W.
7th Floor
Washington, DC 20009
Phone: 202-232-3335
Fax: 202-745-0694
Website: www.publishers.com
President – Patricia Schroeder

Nat'l Ass'n of Broadcasters
1771 N St., N.W.
Washington, DC 20036-2891
Phone: 202-429-5300
Fax: 202-429-5343
Website: www.nba.org
President – Edward Fritts

Nat'l Ass'n of Recording Merchandisers
9 Eves Dr., Suite 120
Marlton, NJ 08053-3138
Phone: 609-596-2221
Fax: 609-596-3268
Email: wooton@narm.com
Website: www.narm.com
President – Pamela Horovitz

Nat'l Ass'n of Video Distributors
700 Frederica St., Suite 205
Owensboro, KY 42301
Phone: 502-926-6002
Fax: 502-685-6080
Exec. Director – Bill Burton

Metal Forming/Fabricating

Fabricators and Manufacturers Ass'n, Int'l
833 Featherstone Road
Rockford, IL 61107
Phone: 815-877-7633
Fax: 815-399-7279
President and CEO
  – John Nandzik, CAE

Precision Metalforming Ass'n
6363 Oak Tree Blvd.
Independence, OH 44131-2500
Phone: 216-901-8800
Fax: 216-901-9190
Email: pma@pma.org
Website: www.pma.org
President – Jon Jenson, CAE

Mining

Nat'l Mining Ass'n
1130 17th St., N.W.
Washington, DC 20036-4677
Phone: 202-463-2651
Fax: 202-857-0135
Website: www.nma.org
President and CEO
  – Gen. Richard L. Lawson,
  USAF (Ret.)

Motor Vehicles

American Automobile Manufacturers Ass'n
1401 H St., N.W., Suite 900
Washington, DC 20005-2110
Phone: 202-326-5500
Fax: 202-326-5567
Website: www.aama.com
President and CEO
  – Andrew H. Card, Jr.

American Bus Ass'n
1100 New York Ave., N.W.
Suite 1050
Washington, DC 20005-3934
Phone: 202-842-1645
Fax: 202-842-0850
Email: abainfo@buses.org
Website: www.buses.org
President – Peter Pantuso

Ass'n of Automotive Aftermarket Distributors
5050 Poplar Ave., Suite 2020
Memphis, TN 38157-2001
Phone: 901-682-9090
Fax: 901-682-9098
Email: partsplus@bellsouth.net
Website: www.partsplus.com
President – Mike Lambert

Automotive Warehouse Distributors Ass'n
9140 Ward Pkwy., Suite 200
Kansas City, MO 64114
Phone: 816-444-3500
Fax: 816-444-0330
Website: www.awda.org
President – Jack Creamer

Internat'l Truck Parts Ass'n
7127 Braeburn Pl.
Bethesda, MD 20817
Phone: 202-544-3090
Fax: 301-229-7331
Exec. Director – Venlo Wolfsohn

Motor and Equipment Manufacturers Ass'n

10 Laboratory Dr.
P.O. Box 13966
Research Triangle Park, NC
27709-3966
Phone: 919-549-4800
Fax: 919-406-1465
President and CEO
  – Robert. R. Miller

Nat'l Truck Equipment Ass'n
37400 Hills Tech Dr.
Farmington Hills, MI
48331-3414
Phone: 810-489-7090
Fax: 810-489-8590
Email: info@ntea.com
Executive Director
  – James D. Carney

Nat'l Truck Leasing System
1 South 450 Summit Ave.
Suite 300
Oak Brook Terrace, IL
60181-3976
Phone: 630-953-8878
Fax: 630-953-0040
Website: www.ntls.com
President – William Ford

Recreation Vehicle Industry Ass'n
1896 Preston White Drive
P.O. Box 2999
Reston, VA 20195
Phone: 703-620-6003
Fax: 703-620-5071
President – David J. Humphreys

Truck Manufacturers Ass'n
1225 New York Ave., N.W.
Suite 300
Washington, DC 20005
Phone: 202-638-7825
Fax: 202-737-3742
Email: tma_dc@ix.netcom.com
Executive Director
  – William Leasure, Jr.

Truck Renting and Leasing Ass'n
1725 Duke St., Suite 600
Alexandria, VA 22314-3457
Phone: 703-299-9120
Fax: 703-299-9115
Email: mpayne@trala.org
Website: www.trala.org
President – J. Michael Payne

Truck Trailer Manufacturers Ass'n
1020 Princess St.
Alexandria, VA 22314-2289
Phone: 703-549-3010
Fax: 703-549-3014
President – Richard P. Bowling

Used Truck Ass'n
600 Reisterstown Road
Suite 404
Baltimore, MD 21208
Phone: 410-602-2470
Fax: 410-486-7478
Website: www.uta.org
Executive Director
 – David A. Kolman

Office Products and Equipment

Business Products Industry Ass'n
301 North Fairfax St.
Alexandria, VA 22314-2696
Phone: 703-549-9040
Fax: 703-683-7552
President – James McGarry

Office Products Wholesalers Ass'n
5024-R Campbell Blvd.
Baltimore, MD 21236-5974
Phone: 410-931-8100
Fax: 410-931-8111
Email: opwa@aol.com
Website: www.opwa.org
Exec. V. President
 – Calvin K. Clemons, CAE

Oil and Gas

American Gas Ass'n
400 North Capitol St., N.W.
Washington, DC 20001
Phone: 703-841-8400
Fax: 703-841-8689
Email: webmaster@aga.com
Website: www.aga.com
President and CEO
 – David N. Parker, CAE

American Petroleum Institute
1220 L St., N.W.
Washington, DC 20005
Phone: 202-682-8000
Fax: 202-682-8115
Website: www.api.org
President – Charles J. DiBona

Gas Processors Ass'n
6526 E. 60th St.
Tulsa, OK 74145-9202
Phone: 918-493-3872
Fax: 918-493-3875
Email: gpa@gasprocessors.com
Website: www.gasprocessors.com
Exec. Director – Mark Sutton

Interstate Natural Gas Ass'n of America
10 G St., N.E., Suite 700
Washington, DC 20002
Phone: 202-216-5900
Fax: 202-216-0877
Website: www.ingaa.org
President – Jerald Halvorsen

Nat'l Petroleum Refiners Ass'n
1899 L. St., N.W,. Suite 1000
Washington, DC 20036
Phone: 202-457-0480
Fax: 202-457-0486
President – Urvan Sternfels

Natural Gas Supply Ass'n
805 15th St., N.W., Suite 510
Washington, DC 20005
Phone: 202-326-9300
Fax: 202-326-9330
Website: www.ngsa.org
President – Nicholas Bush

Petroleum Equipment Institute
6514 East 69th St.
Tulsa, OK 74133-1719
Phone: 918-494-9696
Fax: 918-491-9895
Website: www.pei.org
Exec. V. President
 – Robert Renkes

Packaging

Flexible Packaging Ass'n
1090 Vermont Ave., Suite 500
Washington, DC 20005-4960
Phone: 202-842-3880
Fax: 202-842-3841
Email: fpa@flexpack.org
Website: www.flexpack.org
President – Glenn Braswell

Packaging Machinery Manufacturers Institute
4350 N. Fairfax Drive
Suite 600
Arlington, VA 22203
Phone: 703-243-8555
Fax: 703-243-8556
Website: www.packexpo.com
President – Charles Yuska

Pharmaceutical

Nat'l Ass'n of Pharmaceutical Manufacturers
320 Old Country Road, Rm. 205
Garden City, NY 11530-1752
Phone: 516-741-3699
Fax: 516-741-3696
Email: napmgenrx@aol.com
Website: www.napmnet.org
President – Robert Milanese

Nat'l Pharmaceutical Alliance
421 King St., Suite 222
Alexandria, VA 22314
Phone: 703-836-8816
Fax: 703-549-4749
Website: www.n-p-a.org
President – Christina Sizemore

Nonprescription Drug Manufacturers Ass'n
1150 Connecticut Ave., N.W.
Suite 1200
Washington, DC 20036-4104
Phone: 202-429-9260
Fax: 202-223-6835
President – James Cope

Pharmaceutical Research and Manufacturers of America
1100 15th St., N.W., 9th Floor
Washington, DC 20005
Phone: 202-835-3400
Fax: 202-835-3414
Website: www.phrma.org
President – Alan Holmer

Plastics and Rubber

Rubber Manufacturers Ass'n
1400 K St., N.W., Suite 900
Washington, DC 20005
Phone: 202-682-4800
Fax: 202-682-4854
Website: www.rma.org
President – Donald Shea

Society of the Plastics Industry
1801 K St., N.W., Suite 600-K
Washington, DC 20006-1301
Phone: 202-974-5200
Fax: 202-296-7005
Website: www.socplas.org
President – Larry L. Thomas

Printing

Nat'l Ass'n of Printers and Lithographers
75 West Century Rd.
Paramus, NJ 07652
Phone: 201-342-0700
Fax: 201-634-0325
Website: www.napl.org
President – I. Gregg Van Wert

NPES, the Ass'n for Suppliers of Printing and Publishing Technologies
1899 Preston White Dr.
Reston, VA 20191-4367
Phone: 703-264-7200
Fax: 703-620-0994
Email: npes@npes.org
Website: www.npes.org
President – Regis Delmontagne

Printing Industries of America
100 Daingerfield Rd.
Alexandria, VA 22314
Phone: 703-519-8100
Fax: 703-548-3227
Email: rroper@printing.com
Website: www.printing.com
President – Ray Roper, CAE

Professional Associations

American Purchasing Soc.
430 W. Downer Pl.
Aurora, IL 60506-5035
Phone: 630-859-0250
Fax: 630-859-0270
Email: propurch@aol.com
Website:
www.American-Purchasing.com
President – Harry Hough

American Recovery Ass'n
P.O. Box 6788
New Orleans, LA 70174
Phone: 504-366-7377
Fax: 504-367-6416
Email: ara@repo.org
Website: www.repo.org
Exec. Director – Catherine Rodi

APICS-The Educational Society for Resource Management
500 West Annandale Road
Falls Church, VA 22046-4274
Phone: 703-237-8344
Fax: 703-237-1087
Website: www.apics.org
Executive Director and COO
    – Jeffry W. Raynes, CAE

Ass'n of Machinery and Equipment Appraisers
315 S. Patrick St.
Alexandria, VA 22314
Phone: 703-836-7900
Fax: 703-836-9303
Email: amea@amea.org
Website: www.amea.org
Executive Director
    – Christine V. Druhan

Council of Logistics Management
2805 Butterfield Rd.
Suite 200
Oak Brook, IL 60523
Phone: 630-574-0985
Fax: 630-574-0989
Email: clmadmin@clm1.org
Website: clm1.org
Exec. V. President
    – George Gecowets

Equipment Maintenance Council
P.O. Box 528
Stroud, OK 74079-9013
Phone: 918-968-1077
Phone: 918-968-9621
Email: motherrd@fullnet.net
Website: www.coneq.com
Executive Director
    – Stan Orr, CAE

Financial Executives Institute
10 Madison Avenue
P.O. Box 1938
Morristown, NJ 07962-1938
Phone: 973-898-4600
Fax: 201-538-6144
Fax: pnroy@fei.org
Website: www.fei.org
President – P. Norman Roy

Institute of Management Accountants
10 Paragon Dr.
Montvale, NJ 07645-1760
Phone: 201-573-9000
Fax: 201-573-8185
Website: www.imanet.org
Exec. Director
    – Richard Swanson

Investment Recovery Ass'n
5800 Foxridge Dr., #115
Mission, KS 66202-2333
Phone: 913-262-4597
Fax: 913-262-0174
Email: ira@invrecovery.org
Website: www.invrecovery.org
Executive Director
    – Jane Male, CAE

Nat'l Ass'n of Purchasing Management
2055 East Centennial Circle
P.O. Box 22160
Tempe, AZ 85285-2160
Phone: 602-752-6276
Fax: 602-752-7890
Website: www.napm.org
Executive V. President and COO
    – Paul Novak, CPM

Nat'l Institute of Governmental Purchasing
151 Spring St., Suite 300
Herndon, VA 20170
Phone: 703-736-8900
Fax: 703-736-0644
Website: www.nigp.org
Exec. V. President – Rick Grimm

Sales and Marketing Executives Internat'l
5500 Interstate North Pkwy.,
N.W., Suite 545
Atlanta, GA 30328-4662
Phone: 770-661-8500
Fax: 770-661-8512
Email: smeihq@smei.org
Website: www.smei.org
CEO – Michael Price

Soc. of Manufacturing Engineers
P.O. Box 930
One SME Drive
Dearborn, MI 48121-0930
Phone: 313-271-1500
Fax: 313-271-2861
Website: www.sme.org
Exec. Director – Philip Trimble

Railroads

Ass'n of American Railroads
50 F St., N.W.
Washington, DC 20001-1564
Phone: 202-639-2100
Fax: 202-639-2558
Website: www.aar.org
President – Ed Hamburger

Nat'l Railroad Construction and Maintenance Ass'n
122 C. St., N.W., Suite 850
Washington, DC 20001-2109
Phone: 202-638-7790
Fax: 202-638-1045
Website: www.nrcma.org
President – Kimberly Madigan

Railway Progress Institute
700 N. Fairfax St.
Alexandria, VA 22314-2098
Phone: 703-836-2332
Fax: 703-548-0058
Email: rpi@rpi.org
President – Robert Matthews

Sporting Goods/Recreation

Nat'l Sporting Goods Ass'n
1699 Wall St., Suite 700
Mount Prospect, IL 60056-5780
Phone: 847-439-4000
Fax: 847-439-0111
Email: nsga1699@aol.com
Website: www.nsga.com
President and CEO
– James Faltinek, Ph.D., CAE

Sporting Goods Manufacturers Ass'n
200 Castlewood Dr.
N. Palm Beach, FL 33408-5696
Phone: 561-842-4100
Fax: 561-863-8984
Website: www.sportlink.com
President and CEO
– John D. Riddle

Steel

American Institute of Steel Construction
One E. Wacker Drive
Suite 3100
Chicago, IL 60601-2001
Phone: 312-670-2400
Fax: 312-670-5403
Website: www.aiscweb.org
President – H. Louis Gurthet

American Iron and Steel Institute
1101 17th St., N.W., Suite 1300
Washington, DC 20036-4700
Phone: 202-452-7100
Fax: 202-463-6573
Website: www.steel.org
President and CEO
– Andrew G. Sharkey, III

Ass'n of Steel Distributors
401 N. Michigan Ave.
Chicago, IL 60611-4267
Phone: 312-644-6610
Fax: 312-245-1083
Email: asd@sba.com
Website: www.steeldistributors.org/osd
Exec. Director – Ron Pietrzak

Steel Manufacturers Ass'n
1730 Rhode Island Ave., N.W.
Suite 907
Washington, DC 20036-3101
Phone: 202-296-1515
Fax: 202-296-2506
Email: bechake@steelnet.org
Website: www.steelnet.org
President – James Collins

Stone

Building Stone Institute
P.O. Box 507
Purdys, NY 10578
Phone: 914-232-5725
Fax: 914-232-5259
Exec. V. President
– Dorothy Kender

Nat'l Stone Ass'n
1415 Elliot Pl., N.W.
Washington, DC 20007-2599
Phone: 202-342-1100
Fax: 202-342-0702
Website: www.aggregates.org
President – Jennifer Wilson

Tabletop/Housewares/Gifts

Nat'l Candle Ass'n
1030 15th St., N.W., Suite 870
Washington, DC 20005
Phone: 202-393-2210
Fax: 202-393-0336
Exec. V. President
– Marianne McDermott

Nat'l Housewares Manufacturers Ass'n
6400 Shafer Court, Suite 650
Rosemont, IL 60018-4929
Phone: 847-292-4200
Fax: 847-292-4211
Website: www.housewares.org
Executive Director
– Philip J. Brandl

Nat'l Tabletop and Giftware Ass'n
355 Lexington Ave., 17th Floor
New York, NY 10017-6603
Phone: 212-661-4261
Fax: 212-370-9047
Email: assocmgmt@aol.com
Exec. Director – Peter Rush

Writing Instrument Manufacturers Ass'n
236 Route 38 West, Suite 100
Moorestown, NJ 08057
Phone: 609-231-8500
Fax: 609-231-4664
Email: wima@ahint.com
Exec. V. President
– William MacMillan, III, CAE

Telecommunications

Cable Telecommunications Ass'n
P.O. Box 1005
3950 Chain Bridge Road
Fairfax, VA 22030-1005
Phone: 703-691-8875
Fax: 703-691-8911
Website: www.CATAnet.org
President – Stephen Effros

Cellular Telecommunications Industry Ass'n
1250 Connecticut Ave., N.W.
Suite 700
Washington, DC 20036
Phone: 202-785-0081
Fax: 202-467-6990
Website: www.wow-com.com
President and CEO
– Thomas Wheeler

Nat'l Exchange Carrier Ass'n
100 S. Jefferson Rd.
Whippany, NJ 07981
Phone: 973-884-8000
Fax: 973-884-8469
Website: www.neca.org
President – Bob Anderson

Personal Communications Industry Ass'n
500 Montgomery St., Suite 700
Alexandria, VA 22314-1561
Phone: 703-739-0300
Fax: 703-836-1608
Website: www.pcia.com
President – Emmett Kitchen, Jr.

Telecommunications Industry Ass'n
2500 Wilson Blvd., Suite 300
Arlington, VA 22201-3834
Phone: 703-907-7700
Fax: 703-907-7727
Website: www.tiaonline.org
President – Matthew Flanigan

Toys and Games

Toy Manufacturers of America
1115 Broadway, Suite 400
New York, NY 10010-3303
Phone: 212-675-1141
Fax: 212-633-1429
Website: www.toy.tma.org
President – David Miller

Utilities/Power Generation

American Public Gas Ass'n
11094-D Lee Hwy., Suite 102
Fairfax, VA 22030-5014
Phone: 703-352-3890
Fax: 703-352-1271
Email: bcave@apga.org
Website: www.apga.org
Executive Director
– Robert S. Cave

American Public Power Ass'n
2301 M St., N.W., Suite 300
Washington, DC 20037-1484
Phone: 202-467-2900
Fax: 202-467-2910
Website: www.APPAnet.org
Exec. Director – Alan Richardson

Edison Electric Institute
701 Pennsylvania Ave., N.W.
Washington, DC 20004-2696
Phone: 202-508-5000
Fax: 202-508-5360
Website: www.eei.org
President – Thomas Kuhn, CAE

Nuclear Energy Institute
1776 I St., N.W., Suite 400
Washington, DC 20006-3708
Phone: 202-739-8000
Fax: 202-785-4019
Website: www.nei.org
President – Joe Colvin

Vending Equipment

Nat'l Automatic Merchandising Ass'n
20 North Wacker Dr.
Suite 3500
Chicago, IL 60606-3102
Phone: 312-346-0370
Fax: 312-704-4140
Website: www.vending.org
President – Richard Geerdes

Wholesale/Retail

American Wholesale Marketers Association
1128 16th St., N.W.
Washington, DC 20036-4808
Phone: 202-463-2124
Fax: 202-463-6467
President and CEO
– David E. Strachan, CAE

Associated Surplus Dealers
2950 31st St., Suite 100
Santa Monica, CA 90405
Phone: 310-396-6006
Fax: 310-399-2662
Vice President and Administrator
– Sam Bundy

General Merchandise Distributors Council
1275 Lake Plaza Dr.
Colorado Springs, CO 80906
Phone: 719-576-4260
Fax: 719-576-2661
Email: info@gmdc.org
Website: www.gmdc.org
President – Richard Tilton

Internat'l Mass Retail Ass'n
1700 N. Moore St., Suite 2250
Arlington, VA 22209
Phone: 703-841-2300
Fax: 703-841-1184
Website: www.imra.org
President – Robert Verdisco

Nat'l Ass'n of Chain Drug Stores
413 N. Lee St.
P.O. Box 1417
Alexandria, VA 22313-1480
Phone: 703-549-3001
Fax: 703-836-4869
Website: www.nacds.org
President – Ronald Ziegler

Nat'l Ass'n of Store Fixture Manufacturers
3595 Sheridan St., Suite 200
Hollywood, FL 33021
Phone: 954-893-7300
Fax: 954-893-7500
Email: nasfm@nasfm.org
Website: www.nasfm.org
Exec. Director – Klein Merriman

Nat'l Ass'n of Wholesaler-Distributors
1725 K St., N.W., 3rd Floor
Washington, DC 20006
Phone: 202-872-0885
Fax: 202-785-0586
President – Dirk Van Dongen

Wood/Pulp/Paper

American Forest and Paper Ass'n
1111 19th St., N.W., Suite 800
Washington, DC 20036
Phone: 202-463-2700
Fax: 202-463-2785
Website: www.afandpa.org
CEO – W. Henson Moore

Ass'n of Independent Corrugated Converters
P.O. Box 25708
Alexandria, VA 22313
Phone: 703-836-2422
Fax: 703-836-2795
Email: aicc@aiccbox.org
Website: www.aiccbox.org
Exec. V. President
– Steven Young

Nat'l Hardwood Lumber Ass'n
P.O. Box 34518
Memphis, TN 38184-0518
Phone: 901-377-1818
Fax: 901-382-6419
Email: nhla@natlhardwood.org
Website: www.natlhardwood.org
Exec. Manager
– Paul Houghland, Jr., CAE

North American Wholesale Lumber Ass'n
3601 Algonquin Rd., Suite 400
Rolling Meadows, IL 60008-3108
Phone: 847-870-7470
Fax: 847-870-0201
Website: www.lumber.org
Exec. V. President
– Nicholas Kent

Southern Forest Products Ass'n
P.O. Box 641700
Kenner, LA 70064-1700
Phone: 504-443-4464
Fax: 504-443-6612
Email: klindberg@sfpa.org
Website: www.sfpa.org
President – Karl Lindberg

Timber Products Manufacturers
951 East Third Ave.
Spokane, WA 99202
Phone: 509-535-4646
Fax: 509-534-6106
Email: tpm@tpmrs.com
Website: www.tpmrs.com
General Manager
– Larry Carroll

Appendix B – Why Your Company Should Establish an Asset Recovery Program

Despite the negative financial impact of carrying surplus assets, only a fraction of major companies have allocated dedicated resources to asset recovery.

The Investment Recovery Association is an international, non-profit trade association that promotes the study, development and implementation of techniques to improve dispositioning of surplus assets. A recent benchmark study among major companies conducted by the Center for Advanced Purchasing Studies, in conjunction with the Investment Recovery Association, found the following:

- There was only one Investment Recovery (IR) professional for every 7,155 company employees.

- Average benefit provided by each IR employee was $1.7 million.

- Ratio of gross revenue to operating expense from asset recovery was 15:1.

- Average gross revenues per IR transaction was $30,849 vs. average operating expense per transaction of $1,680.[9]

In addition, the Investment Recovery Association has found that:

- 70-90% of every dollar generated by investment recovery goes to bottom line as profit.[10]

Ralston Purina Company, an Association member, estimates that its asset recovery program contributed $15 million to the bottom line over an eight-year period.[11]

What's the moral of the story? It seems clear that establishing a focused asset recovery program can greatly improve your company's financial results.

For more information on how to establish an investment recovery program at your company, contact the Investment Recovery Association at 913-262-4597 or via email at ira@invrecovery.org. Also visit the Association website at www.invrecovery.org.

[9] Center for Advanced Purchasing Studies, Purchasing Performance Benchmarks, 1997 data, published 1999
[10] Investment Recovery Association
[11] Food Formulating Magazine, February 1996

Appendix C – How to Become a Certified Manager of Investment Recovery

If you are already employed as an investment recovery professional you may apply for the Investment Recovery Association's Certified Manager of Investment Recovery (CMIR) designation.

You'll join a select group of professionals who have made the commitment to excellence in investment recovery management. The CMIR designation provides professional recognition and greater earning potential, as well as the satisfaction that you have attained one of the highest levels of achievement in your profession.

Investment recovery professionals who meet the following criteria are eligible:

- At least three years of experience

- Acceptable character, ability and reputation

- Member of Investment Recovery Association

- Pledge in writing to adhere to the Association code of ethics

- Score of 35 points on Personal Data Form

- Score of 35 points on written exam administered by the Association. (The Association provides a CMIR Review prior to exams, and also offers a CMIR study guide for the exam.)

For more information on obtaining the CMIR designation, contact the Investment Recovery Association at 913-262-4597 or visit the Association website at www.invrecovery.org.

Appendix D – How to Become Certified in Production and Inventory Management

For professionals in the area of manufacturing and distribution planning and control, the designation of Certified in Production and Inventory Management (CPIM) is recognized worldwide as the highest standard of competence in resource management.

The CPIM designation is conferred by APICS – The Educational Society for Resource Management. APICS is an international, not-for-profit organization that has been serving the manufacturing and service sectors since 1957. Its 70,000 members represent 20,000 diverse companies worldwide.

Since the program's inception in 1973, more than 60,000 professionals have earned APICS' CPIM designation, which identifies them as specialists in production and inventory management. The designation certifies that they have demonstrated high levels of expertise and skill, and it provides enhanced credibility with employers and customers.

The CPIM preparation course teaches critical skills in the design, operation and control of systems for the manufacture and distribution of products, including:

- accurate forecasting for streamlined operations
- enhanced supply chain management
- just-in-time delivery of products and services
- performance maximization of systems and technologies

The seven curriculum modules include Basics of Supply Chain Management, Inventory Management, Material and Capacity Requirements Planning, Master Planning, Production Activity and Control, Just-in-Time, and Systems and Technologies.

There is a comprehensive exam for each of the modules, and a candidate earns the CPIM designation after passing the exam for at least six of the modules. You need not be an APICS member to become certified, but members do receive a discount on exam registration fees and reference materials.

For more information about APICS and the CPIM designation, contact APICS at 800-444-2742 or visit their website at www.apics.org.

CPIM

Brin McCagg is the Chief Executive Officer of TradeOut.com. He founded the company in August 1998. Mr. McCagg started his career in corporate finance at Drexel Burnham Lambert. After receiving his MBA from the Wharton School in 1990, he started his own company, Full Circle/Environmental Technologies Inc., which recycled PCBs from electrical equipment and later CFCs from commercial air conditioning units. Mr. McCagg built the firm into a $60 million NASDAQ listed company before selling his interest in late 1997.

Special thanks to Andy Kantor and all employees of TradeOut.com for their assistance in the preparation of this Guide.